In the Name of Allah,

The Compassionate, the Merciful

THE WINE OF LOVE

Mystical Poetry of Imam Khomeini

Translators

Dr. Ghulam-Rida A'wani

and

Dr. Muhammad Legenhausen

Introduced and Annotated by:

Dr. Muhammad Legenhausen

The Institute for the Compilation and Publication
of Imam Khomeini's Works
(International Affairs Department)

Table of Contents

Preface

Imam Khomeini, may his soul be sanctified, was a person who, by his auspicious presence in the world of modern coercion and deception, voiced the slogan of awakening and through his noble message that had the fragrant aroma of the true breeze of monotheism, showed the path to those who had gone astray, and as among the decanters of love which had enraptured himself, he served mouthfuls to those who thirst for love and truth.

Centuries passed and the dormant earth remained expectant until the alma mater of times graduated a son such as Khomeini, a man who was a guide to the path of truth and demonstrator of the path of love and religion. Islam had remained covered under the veils of deception imposed on it by tyrants and rulers dispensing coercion and cruelty. These enemies of human happiness and salvation had concealed the beautiful face of Islam until a man rose and, through a power that arose from faith in Almighty God and his own true devotion, wiped off the dust and taught the Muslims what the true rusts of the face of Islam were and how, by manly uprising and valiant *jihad*, Islam could be saved from the pestilence in which it was engulfed.

Verily, why was Imam Khomeini promoted to such a station and become the bright sun that no bat could tolerate?

Truly, if this wasn't the case, the rulers of the East and the West and their reactionary hired agents during his blissful life when his divine guardianship, as the shadow of the heavenly tree of Tuba, sheltered men everywhere on earth, and after his ascension would not undertake such extensive challenge to an epic man showing the road to salvation!

The cause for so much honor and dignity is embodied in one sentence: Imam Khomeini was assimilated in Allah and the divine religion of Islam. Martyr Sayyid Muhammad Baqir as-Sadr[1] has mentioned this nicely: "Melt away in Imam Khomeini even as he had melted away in Islam."

From your cask has come the drunkenness of the heart-lost lover;

---

[1] The great Muslim scholar and jurist, Ayatullah al-'Uzma Sayyid Muhammad Baqir as-Sadr, was born in 1931/1350 AH to a prominent family in Kazimayn, a city in Iraq. He first studied at the Najaf seminary and by the age of twenty he attained the status of theologian and obtained the qualifications to practice religious jurisprudence. He was active in most Islamic movements and in a famous decree, he banned membership in the Ba'ath Party of Iraq and declared the members of this party as outright enemies of Islam and the Muslims. In another decree he proclaimed as martyrs those who fought and were slain in the Islamic Revolution of Iran against the Shah's regime. In the month of Jamad al-Awwal 1400 AH (April 8, 1980), the Ba'ath government of Iraq martyred him and his sister after months of imprisonment and torture. He wrote numerous books, the most famous of which are *Falsafatuna* ("Our Philosophy") and *Iqtisaduna* ("Our Economics").

For the English translation of the two mentioned books, see Muhammad Baqir as-Sadr, Our Philosophy (Muhammadi Trust, n.d.), http://al-islam.org/philosophy; Our Economics (Tehran: World Organization for Islamic Services, 1982). (Eds.)

Preface

The outcome of my life is this drunkenness, no other.
If between you and Him, besides you stands none else.
If you are a heart-lost lover, abandon yourself.

That is how he (Imam Khomeini) has acknowledged life
and all that has being and existence. He considered man's
worth and credibility in his seeing another but God and
interpreted man's liberty to mean that he is tied to the
beloved's tress and ringlet and see nothing nor be mindful of
anything save the One and Only Divinity.

I am nothing, nothing,
*   for being is all in naught.*
Nothing else but nothing,
*   for You gaze upon the naught.*

During the course of his blessed life, Imam Khomeini
presented to humanity, by his pen and tongue, all he had
received from the divine source of grace. He wrote books,
delivered sermons, wrote messages and, in his everlasting will
and testament, he penned the final chapter of his guiding life.
In all these the Imam has tried to speak in the language of the
folks or his audience as called for by his station of
guardianship and leadership. Had he spoken in his own tongue
revealing the concealed secrets, none could understand. Imam

Ja'far as-Sadiq[2] (*'a*) has said that the Prophet (s) never in his life time addressed the people in his own tongue.

In like manner, in his divine mystic, peripatetic journeys Imam Khomeini had gained access to secrets that were concealed from others. Some of those secrets found manifestation in the glorious guardianship of this noble personality, while others are reflected in the ardent, impassionate and stirring odes and lyric poetry of His Eminence.

Imam Khomeini's poetry are indeed the hidden secrets between him and that Unique Friend the friend for whose love only the Imam lived, who was all that he could see and acknowledge and to whose command alone he would bow.

I will be a moth, burning,
burning all my life in her candle.
I will be drunk with wine,
marveling at her beautiful face.

---

[2]Ja'far ibn Muhammad ('a) entitled, as-Sadiq (The Truthful)," is the sixth Imam from the Prophet's Progeny (83-148 AH). Many of the Sunni and Shi'ah 'ulama and scholars attended his teaching classes and seminars. Narrators of tradition have quoted the number of Imam as-Sadiq's students as four thousand. The socio-economic conditions of his time necessitated greatest efforts to be made by His Holiness in the areas of expanding authentic and original Islamic teachings and in the training and education of faithful students. For this reason the books of tradition and other books quote and cite more traditions from Imam Ja'far as-Sadiq than from any other infallible Imams.

If he tolerated derisions by the ignorant; if he took poison and traded his pride,[3] it was for Islam and Allah and if he waged jihad, that too, was to please the Lord. In his ode known as the 'Alawiyyah Elegy, Ibn Abi'l-Hadid[4] has said:

For love's sake the veil
  of chastity I'll tear.
Infamy, should the friend's path entail
  is the loveliest thing to bear.

That is how one should be in incurring the pleasure of the friend. As a noble tradition implies, a believer does not fear the blame of the reproaches.

From a single view, the poetry of Imam Khomeini is a compendium of all the qualities and aspects of his personality. For, his turbulent spirit has visited all corners and horizons, and the lights of his personality have radiated in all stations. At the same time, the Imam's poetry comprise his only unspoken secrets for which there was no audience in this

---

[3]In his message of July 20, 1988, commemorating the anniversary of the Meccan Massacre and his acceptance of the Security Council's Resolution 598, Imam Khomeini said: "The acceptance of this resolution is more lethal for me than any poison but I seek the consent of the Lord... In the hope of incurring His pleasure and mercy, I disregarded what I had said and, if I had any honor, I traded it with Almighty God."

[4]'Izzaddin 'Abdul-Hamid, known as Ibn Abi'l-Hadid" was a statesman of the Abbasid Dynasty and a literary figure and historian (586-655 AH). His major work is the *SharhNahj al-Balaghah,* a commentary of the *Nahj al-Balaghah* (Peak of Eloquence) (a compendium of Imam 'Ali's ('a) sermons, letters, and maxims).A full-length English translation and commentary on the *Nahj al-Balaghah* is available on-line at http://al-islam.org/nahjul/index.htm (Eds.)

world, for only words could withstand the weight of such unfathomable mysteries. Words are divine blessing for mankind, and God's relations with men are through words. Words were a "well" for him to put his head, as in the case of Hadrat 'Ali ('*a*), and whisper his hidden secrets to it. This is how Imam Khomeini's verses found form and how he occasionally composed some poetry.

Since the poetry of Imam are gnostic in expression and meaning and his mystic personality was infinite, his lyric poems and odes have multiple strata, and each reader enjoys this ocean of insight and meaning according to his capacity of understanding. The spiteful, ignorant and uncultured enemy who naturally has very scant knowledge and understanding of these concepts and takes them to mean as he thinks, regards the term, love, in these poems to mean as what the vulgar think of it, and the term, Friend, is taken to mean what the vulgar consider it to mean.

While the divine prophets were persecuted by ignorant persons and deceitful enemies or even murdered by them and the Seal of the prophets (s) were called by such elements as "crazy," "magician," "poet," etc., it is not surprising if the ignoble, spiteful individuals interpret the lofty words of Imam Khomeini in any way they want.

Verily, those who understand themselves are ever so few!

On the other hand, those who enjoy the delicacy of "the jug of love" and divine knowledge, search for perfection, and understand the term, hijab (veil, barrier), tear it and soar above the subterfuge of the meanings of words and immerse in the tumultuous depths of these poems, find them engulfed with the impassioned love of a servant (of God) who has rested his head at the threshold of the "Beloved" or "Friend" and wants nothing but Him. Such is the worship of the noble and free minds:

I will rest my head on her feet,
  kissing them 'till the instant of death.
I will be drunk with the wine of her jug
  'till the morning of the resurrection.

Thus, words, which are the most potent and abstract form of realization of the meanings and of setting forth the facts that is why poetry is said to be the most abstract form of art can themselves be *hijab* or barriers for the comprehension of the concepts.

The deeper and more exact the meaning and the heavier the moral burden of the speaker of words, the more the barriers to them. In addition to their apparent meanings, words have inner chambers and it takes a highly skillful driver to tear up the veils and roam around from one chamber to another.

Due to its depth and richness of meanings derived from Islam, one of the characteristics of Persian mystical poetry is that meanings do not only appear on the surface of words. In fact, mystic words and terms are all used figuratively and their real meanings are concealed. Man better understands reality through allegory.

In the Holy Qur'an, wherever Almighty God speaks of Hell and Heaven, for closer comprehension by minds, He uses the names of objects that men recognize such as palaces, trees, streams, beautiful women, silk cloth, honey, fire, etc. Whereas the Hereafter, is not like this world bound by matter, and things that are there differ from things that are here on earth. And since this world is figurative in relation to the Hereafter, these objects are all used allegorically.

The core and axis of mysticism is "love," and when love comes to the fore, a lover and a beloved enter the picture and, when the poet wants to speak of the "heart-burnt lover" (whose heart has been burned by love's flame) and the tantalizing beloved and draw pictures of them, he is impelled to use whatever metaphor, comparison, allusion, and such figurative terms existing in his own language, and in this way, interpret the real love the object of which is the infinite Truth and the One-and-Only God. The poet has no other elements available to him and is obliged to make use of exoteric and real elements for stating and expressing the meanings of lofty esoteric concepts, and thus, span a bridge between matter and sense, exterior and interior, real and figurative.

It must be said that the process of the creation of the world is also in this manner and man's progressive course from the world of matter to heaven, from material to moral and beyond matter towards perfection takes place in the similar fashion. If it wasn't so, man's movement and the progression of the world and perfection would all be meaningless:

I am a supplicant for a goblet of wine
*   From the hand of a sweetheart.*
In whom can I confess this secret of mine,
*   Where can I take this sorrow?*
I have lost my soul in despair
*   of seeing the face of the Friend.*
I am the rue, whose burnt scent fills the air,
*   I am the moth 'round the candle.*

Who is there to understand the depth of these words? He (the Imam) was being consumed in the flame of divine love and was feeling the ecstasy of that wine which God has promised His true servants in heaven. For such a man, this world is nothing but a tight cage and his only wish is joining that "Friend".

The criterion for his attachment to objects is love for Allah. Whatever has a color and aroma like that of the Friend is beautiful for him and anything that is not reminiscent of the Friend is redundant for him. Even the mosque, the minaret, the school and the books, if they are without Him and His ardent love, are null and void. This is so because in a monotheistic logic like this, nothing is real except Him and whatever can serve as a bridge to the Friend must be adhered to and whatever is not like this, is null and void and must be relinquished. **"I have set my face towards Him who created the heavens and the earth."**[5]

I did not find purity in the session of the dervishes.
   Within the cloister, I heard none call on Him.
I did not find the Friend in the books of the seminary.
   At the top of the minaret, I saw no sound of the Beloved.
I did not uncover anything in any scholarly books.
In the lessons of Scripture, I was led nowhere.
I spent my life in the temple, spent my life in vain.
   Among my companions, I found neither cure nor affliction.
To the circle of the lovers I would go, and there I find
   a breeze from the garden of a sweetheart, and footprints.

He, who is fascinated and captivated by His Countenace, shuns anything that is not of Him. He disowns the *I*'s and the we's, and avoids the circles of friends, rivals, the mystic's circle, the mosque, and the school, and searches for a refuge, away from all these, to be alone with Him and Him only and

---

[5] Qur'an 6:79.

be so befuddled by His love as to "forget" himself entirely and "forget" all else. It is at this point that he (the Imam) hymns:

Open the door of the tavern before me night and day,
  for I have become weary of the mosque and seminary.

And

  O You saqi! Fill up my cup
  With wine to cleanse my soul!
  For my soul is overflowing,
  Flowing over with passion for fame.
  Fill up my cup with the wine
  Which annihilates this soul,
  Which expels the cope of intrigue
  And my well-laid traps from being.

Even knowledge and gnosticism become hijab (veil, barrier) for him who sees and seeks nothing but the Truth (God) and he wants to tear up this veil, too, because knowledge and '*irfan* are holy only if they can be a road to Him, otherwise, they have no per se value:

In the tavern, learning and mysticism have no way,
  For in the station of the lovers, fallacy has no way.

  And

When from the gnostic realm I came,
I saw all that had been in vain,
All that we'd heard or studied of,
Was vain, after I came to love.

While all regard gnosticism as the only road to reach Him, he (Imam Khomeini) is so monotheistic that he even sees *'irfan* as a barrier and declares it null and void. He wants the plain Truth, and since the bare Truth is nothing but the sacred Essence of the Friend, everything else is null and void.

Imam Khomeini's poetry, as in the case of the personality of that great and magnanimous man, is stormy and effervescent. Albeit a love poetry, it is replete with the spirit of valiance, nobility and epic. In loving God, he is gallant, brave and fearless. He carries his own gallows and like Mansur (al-Hallaj)[6] cries out: *"Ana al-Haqq"* (I am the Truth!) even if he would be hanged (as al-Hallaj was).

I have departed from myself,
Beating the drum of "I am the Truth!"
I have become like Mansur,
a buyer of a hanging rope.

We are entangled in plurality while he is captivated by the mole of the Beloved or Friend's lip, the mole which is the

---

[6]See note 40, p. 30 of the present book. (Eds.)

central point of being's domain and the focal point of monotheism. We are sickly because of our carnal desires while he is befuddled by the Friend's (eye) vision and insight which oversees the secrets of all that is apparent and all that is concealed, and if that "eye" shows favor to a person he shall become ensnared, enthralled and enraptured. We are ensnared by the unreal, untrue objects. We do not see the Truth. We do not comprehend the beauty of the Friend. If we could we should surely become "beset" by it.

We are beset by the idol of *nafs* or carnal desire and the worldly idols we ourselves have created. He is captivated by that unique idol, the One and Only Friend and Master. We are concerned with thoughts of our shame and dishonor while he is free and rid of all that is lust and shame. We are caught in the meanings of words and interpretation of terms while he is beset by the love to see the beauties of the Friend. He had shed away the robe of existence and attained union with the Friend and has saddened us by his ascension. We see the world of matter and material and he is witnessing the Heaven. In the words of Ibn Abi al-Hadid:

Patience is nice
not in separation from thee.
Hardships will all ease
except sorrow on account of thee.

The present volume is Dr. Ghulam-Rida A'wani and Dr. Muhammad Legenhausen's English rendition of the Persian book, *Badeh-ye 'Ishq* (The Wine of Love), which is a collection of Imam Khomeini's mystical poetry with the appendage of the eight *ghazal* poems in an earlier and smaller collection, *Sabu-ye 'Ishq* (The Jug of Love)[7] as well as Prof. Legenhausen's *On the Symbolism of Religious Poetry*[8] as appendix.

International Affairs Department
The Institute for Compilation and Publication of Imam Khomeini's Works

August 2002

---

[7] Imam Khomeini, A Jug of Love, tr. Muhammad Legenhausen and 'Abdul-'Azim Sarvdalir (Tehran: The Islamic Thought Foundation, 1994). (Eds.)

[8] *Ibid.*, pp. 27-32. (Eds.)

Translator's Introduction

In the name of Allah, the Compassionate, the Merciful

I went to Tehran to study Islamic Philosophy, and to teach Contemporary Western Philosophy of Religion at the Islamic Academy of Philosophy of Iran in the fall of 1990, but I was also interested in the poetry of Imam Khomeini, may he rest in peace. Though there had been rumors, it did not become generally known that Imam had written poetry until after he had passed away.

Less than three weeks after Imam's death on June 4, 1989, his son, Hujjat al-Islam Sayyid Ahmad, offered one of his father's poems to the Iranian public through its publication in a Tehran newspaper, Kayhan. In the September 4, 1989 edition of the New Republic magazine, an English rendition of the poem first published in Kayhan appeared by the great scholar and translator, William Chittick. I visited Prof. Chittick in his office at the University of New York at Stony Brook and asked him about Imam's poetry, but he told me that he had only translated that one poem.

The mystical nature of the poem caught many, even among Imam's most ardent devotees, by surprise. In one couplet, Imam wrote, "Open the door of the tavern and let us go there day and night, For I am sick and tired of the mosque and seminary."

The surprise is generated by the contradiction between the literal and symbolic uses of the images. Imam Khomeini was a great supporter of the religious institutions of the mosque and seminary, but in the poetic genre of which his poem is an instance, the mosque and the seminary are symbols for insincerity and pretentiousness. Before going to Iran, when I visited the Ambassador of Iran to the United Nations, Dr. Kamal Kharrazi,[*] he had taken a framed and beautifully decorated piece of calligraphy from the wall and revealed to me that this was a poem composed by Imam, and explained some of what it meant. It seemed to be some sort of love poem in which highly stylized romantic imagery was used to express a mystical devotion to God.

After I settled in Tehran, I started asking people about Imam's poetry. They seemed surprised that I should be interested. I went to a bookstore right outside the gate of the University of Tehran and told a salesman there that I wanted to read the poetry of Imam Khomeini. He smiled and gave me

---

[*] Dr. Kamal Kharrazi is presently the Foreign Minister of the Islamic Republic of Iran. (Eds.)

a slender green volume, and asked where I was from. "America," I said. "And you are Muslim?" "Praise Allah!"

The young revolutionaries with their short thin beard grinned in wonder that an American Muslim was in Tehran and wanted to read the poetry of Imam Khomeini. They wished me well and gave me a small photograph of Imam being kissed by his grandson. This was not the image of 'the Ayatullah' with which Americans had become familiar during what was called 'the hostage crisis' in the US, and the 'spy crisis' in Iran, nor was it the image of the revolutionary leader, 'the hope of the oppressed people of the world,' which had been presented by the Iranian media.

The poetry, like that photograph, offered a glimpse into an intensely personal aspect of the life of Imam Khomeini, an aspect which even now, more than two years after Imam's departure, has largely remained veiled from the English speaking world.

The poet and mystic, Ruhullah Musawi Khomeini, was born in 1902 in the town of Khomein, which is about half way between Tehran and the southwestern city of Ahwaz. Ruhullah's father and grandfather were religious scholars in Khomein. His father, Ayatullah Mustafa, is said to have been murdered by bandits when Ruhullah was less than six months old. His mother, Hajar, was the daughter of the religious scholar Aqa Mirza Ahmad Mujtahid Khwansari. The boy was raised by his mother and an aunt, both of whom died of cholera when he was six. His education was then supervised by his older brother, Ayatullah Pasandideh.

At nineteen, Ruhullah traveled northwest from Khomein to the city of Arak, where he became a student of Shaykh 'Abd al-Karim Ha'eri, a leading religious scholar of his day. The following year, Shaykh Ha'eri and his student Ruhullah moved to Qum, where the Shaykh reorganized and revitalized the entire institution of religious education in that city, which was already famous as a center of learning. Ruhullah studied in Qum until the death of Shaykh Ha'eri, in 1936, after which he began teaching theology, ethics, philosophy, and mysticism.

It was during his first fourteen years in Qum that Ayatullah Khomeini became familiar with the intertwined traditions of philosophy and mysticism which flourished during Iran's Safawid period (16th and 17th centuries) and which continue to exert an enormous influence on contemporary Shi'ite thought.

When he arrived in Qum, Imam Khomeini began to receive private instruction in ethics with Haj MirzaJawad Maleki Tabrizi, the author of a book entitled, The *Secrets of Prayer (Asrar as-Salat)*, Imam Khomeini also wrote a book on this topic, called The *Secret of Prayer: Prayers of the Gnostics or Ascension of the Wayfarers (Sirr as-Salat: Salat al-'Arifin ya*

Mi'raj as-Salikin). His instruction under Mirza Jawad continued until the death of the teacher, in 1925.

Imam Khomeini also studied the mystic traditions from Haj Mirza Abu'l-Hasan Rafi'i Qazvini, who was in Qum from 1923 to 1927. Qazvini is known for his commentary on a supplication which is recited daily in the pre-dawn hours during the month of Ramadan. Later, Imam Khomeini would also write a commentary on this prayer. Finally, and perhaps most importantly among his spiritual guides, there was Aqa Mirza Muhammad 'Ali Shahabadi, the author of *Spray from the Seas (Rashahat al-Bahar)*, who was in Qum from 1928 to 1935.

In the mystic tradition of which Shahabadi was a part, the phrase 'spray from the sea' may be taken as a symbol for inspiration from God. It was with Shahabadi that Imam Khomeini is reported to have studied the *Fusus al-Hikam* (The Bezels of Wisdom) of Ibn al-'Arabi (d. 1240) and the important commentary on that work by Qaysari (d. 1350).[1]

In 1929, Imam Khomeini married, and a year later his first son, Mustafa, was born. Over the course of the years, two other sons and four daughters were born. Mustafa would grow up to be killed in Iraq by agents of the Shah. The youngest

---

[1]The *Fusus al-Hikam* has been translated by R.W.J. Austin as The Bezels of Wisdom (New York: The Paulist Press, 1980).

son, Sayyid Ahmad, would become a secretary to his father, and afterward, a political leader in his own right.

Recalling his years as a student in Qum, Imam Khomeini himself has publicly commented on the hostility toward mysticism and philosophy which was to be found in certain quarters in Qum, feelings which are still harbored by some members of the clergy.[2] The story is often repeated that when Imam had begun teaching philosophy in Qum and his first son was a small child, some seminarians felt it necessary to perform a ritual cleansing of a cup from which the child had drunk water because of his impurity as the son of a teacher of philosophy! Imam reports that his teacher, Shahabadi, sought to oppose this hostility by making people familiar with the doctrines of the mystics so they could see for themselves that there was nothing inimical to Islam in the teachings of the gnostics:

Once a group of merchants came to see the late Shahabadi (may God have mercy on him), and he began to speak to them on the same mystical topics that he taught to everyone. I asked him whether it was appropriate to speak to them of such matters and he replied: "Let them be exposed just once to these heretical teachings! I too now find it incorrect to divide

---

[2]See Imam's lectures on *Surah al-Fatihah* in Islam and Revolution, tr. Hamid Algar (Berkeley: Mizan Press, 1981), p. 424.

people into categories and pronounce some incapable of understanding these matters."[3]

One of the most dramatic efforts of Imam Khomeini to bring mysticism to the people occurred after the Islamic Revolution with his Lectures on Surah al-*Fatihah* from which the above report has been quoted. After the Revolution, there were televised lessons on the interpretation of the Qur'an by Ayatullah Taleqani. When Ayatullah Taleqani died on September 10, 1979, about a half year after the victory of the revolution, the televised commentary on the Qur'an was taken up by a younger scholar. Imam Khomeini suggested that a more senior authority might be sought for the program.

After consulting among themselves, those responsible for the broadcast decided to request that Imam himself provide the commentary. Imam responded that if the cameras could be brought to his residence he would comply with the request. The result was the Lectures on *Surah al-Fatihah*, a stunning mystical interpretation of the opening verses of the Qur'an, in which one of the dominant themes was the claim that the whole world is a name of God.

In these lectures Imam also contends that the philosophers of Islam, the mystics and the poets have used different terminologies to express the same insights, and he urges his

---

[3]*Ibid.*, p. 425.

viewers not to reject what is taught by members of these groups until they understand what is being expressed, even if the language used raises suspicions of heterodoxy. Thus, Imam's preaching in this area was very much a plea for tolerance.

Imam Khomeini's emphasis on tolerance was not limited to mysticism and poetry. Imam Khomeini's teacher in Islamic jurisprudence, Shaykh Ha'eri, was succeeded in Qum by Ayatullah Burujerdi, who came to be recognized as the supreme authority on the subject. After the death of Ayatullah Burujerdi, in 1961, Imam Khomeini came to be recognized as one of several supreme experts in Islamic jurisprudence, a *marja'-e taqlid*. In this role, Imam Khomeini issued a number of decrees which were looked upon with suspicion by more conservative clerics.

Many of the religious scholars in both Sunni and Shi'ite legal schools have ruled that music and chess are forbidden activities. Imam Khomeini ruled that some forms of music are permissible and that playing chess is not contrary to Islamic law. As a result, interest in traditional Iranian music has thrived since the Revolution. Imam Khomeini has also encouraged women to play an expanded role in society, to the chagrin of more conservative interpreters of Islamic law.

To Western observers it may seem paradoxical that the very same man who preached tolerance with respect to the perceived challenges to orthodoxy posed by philosophy, mysticism, poetry, and music, should also have been so intolerant toward the proponents of Westernization, toward the form of Marxism propagated in the name of Islam by the Mujahiden Khalq Organization (MKO), and toward those who, like Salman Rushdie, would insult the Prophet of Islam or his family.

The apparent contradiction is removed once it is recognized that Imam Khomeini did not value tolerance for its own sake, but for the sake of Islam. Central to Imam Khomeini's understanding of Islam is gnosis, *'irfan*. In Sunni Islam, the exoteric and esoteric dimensions of religion have been kept largely distinct, with the esoteric mostly confined to the Sufi orders. In Shi'ite Islam, there has been a long tradition in which many of the practices and teachings of the Sufis have been integrated into the religious life and thought of an important segment of the official clergy.

Those form of mysticism, or gnosis, draws upon the Sufi theory of Ibn al-'Arabi,[4] the philosophical mysticism of Sadr

---

[4] Muhyi ad-Din ibn al-'Arabi, the celebrated Muslim mystic whose influence came to permeate the intellectual and spiritual life of virtually the entire Muslim world, was born at Murcia in Southern Spain in 1165. Much of his youth was spent in Seville, where he devoted himself to literary, theological and mystical studies. After visiting Granada and other Spanish towns, as well as Tunis, Fez, and Morocco, he set out in 1202 for the East by way of Egypt, whence he made the pilgrimage to Mecca. He did not return to Spain. Many of the remaining years of his life were passed in the

ad-Din Shirazi[5] (d. 1640) and Hadi Sabzewari[6] (d. 1878), both of whom were Shi'ite clerics, and the poetic expression of

---

neighborhood of Mecca, but he also traveled extensively to Babylonia, Asia Minor, and Syria, everywhere gaining disciples and spreading his doctrines through dialogues with scientists and scholars.

Whether we regard the extent of his theological writings or their influence on the subsequent development of Islamic mysticism, Ibn al-'Arabi can justly claim the supreme position among Sufi authors which posterity has accorded him, and which is attested by the title, Ash-Shaykh al-Akbar, conferred on him by the almost unanimous voice of those who are best qualified to judge. The list of his works drawn up by himself contains 289 titles, and some of them are of enormous length. The most famous and important is the *Futuhat al-Makkiyah*. In this, as in many of his works, Ibn al-'Arabi professes to communicate mysteries revealed to him in ecstatic vision by prophets, angels, and even God Himself. (Pub.)

[5]Sadr ad-Din Shirazi (d. 1050 AH/1640), better known as Mulla Sadra, was a philosopher who led the Iranian cultural renaissance in the 17th century. The foremost representative of *Ishraqi (Illuminationist)* School of philosopher-mystics, he is commonly regarded by Iranians as the greatest philosopher of Iran. A scion of a notable Shirazi family, Mulla Sadra completed his education in Isfahan, then the leading cultural and intellectual center of Iran. After his studies with scholars there, he produced several works, the most famous of which was his *Asfar* (Journeys). *Asfar* contains the bulk of his philosophy, which was influenced by a personal mysticism bordering on the asceticism that he experienced during a 15-year retreat at *Kahak*, a village near Qum in Iran.

Toward the end of his life, Mulla Sadra returned to Shiraz to teach. His teachings, however, were considered heretical by the orthodox Shi'ite theologians, who persecuted him, though his powerful family connections permitted him to continue to write. He died on a pilgrimage to Mecca. (Pub.)

[6]Hajji Hadi Sabzewari (1797-1878) was the philosopher and poet noted for disseminating and clarifying the doctrines of Mulla Sadra. The Qajar Shah Nasir ad-Din ordered a mausoleum to be built for him at Mashhad. (Pub.)

mysticism by Mawlawi Jalal ad-Din ar-Rumi[7](d. 1273) and Hafiz.[8](d. 1391). The poetry is often set to music. Because of political and religious repression, those involved in '*irfan* often had to keep their teachings underground. Imam Khomeini, in line with sentiments his reports having been expressed by his teacher Shahabadi, sought to initiate a process through which '*irfan* could become public. This process was not to be a sudden revolution. His own works on 'irfan were not very widely distributed during his lifetime, but a persistent emphasis on the mystical elements of Shi'te thought were interspersed among the more popular political declaration, and may be found in The *Greatest Jihad*,[9] as well.

The revolutionary Islamic movement led by Imam Khomeini may even be viewed as the exoteric dimension of the impetus to reveal Islamic mysticism to the public. The Islamic revolution was a means to bring Islam into public life, from which it was being marginalized during the reign of the Shah. The process of making Islam central to public life was

---

[7]Mawlawi Jalal ad-Din ar-Rumi (1207-1273) was the greatest mystic poet in the Farsi language and founder of the Mawlawiyyah order of dervishes ("The Whirling Dervishes"). He is famous for his lyrics and for his didactic epic, Spiritual Couplets. (Pub.)

[8]Khwajah Shams ad-Din Muhammad Hafiz Shirazi (ca. 1325-1391) was the fourteenth century Persian lyric bard and panegyrist, and commonly considered as the preeminent master of the *ghazal* form. (Pub.)

[9]Imam Khomeini, The Greatest Jihad: Combat with the Self, 2nd ed., tr. Muhammad Legenhausen (Tehran: The Institute for Compilation and Publication of Imam Khomeini's Works, 2003). (Eds.)

also resisted by conservative religious groups, who saw in this movement a departure from tradition.

Imam Khomeini argued that the guardian jurist of Islamic law had the authority to modify the traditional understanding of the law in order to protect the Islamic order. Conservatives would argue that any break from tradition could only bring deviation from Islamic order. The kind of judgment required by Imam Khomeini's vision of Islamic government is one which goes beyond what is provided for in traditional discussions of Islamic jurisprudence. It is a kind of wisdom, however, which can be expected of the 'perfect man', the *insan kamil*, the goal of personal development in the mystic tradition.

An example of the way in which his political awareness demanded a tolerance not found among more conservative clerics may be found in his attitudes toward Sunni Islam. In traditional Shi'ite circles it would not be considered permissible for a Shi'ite to stand behind a Sunni prayer leader. Imam Khomeini ruled that such prayer was valid, and even himself publicly participated in ritual prayer behind a Sunni cleric.

Thus, the flexibility and tolerance which characterized Imam Khomeini's thought do not stem from the libertarian element in Islamic thought, but from a commitment to a movement from the esoteric to exoteric dimensions of Islamic life, a movement which demanded the implementation of Islamic law as well as the propagation of mystical ideas.

Imam Khomeini's attitudes toward mysticism and politics are especially well illustrated by his invitation to President Gorbachev to embrace Islam. On January 7, 1989, Imam Khomeini sent a delegation to Moscow led by Ayatullah Jawad Amuli who presented Imam's letter of invitation to President Gorbachev.[10]

In the letter, Imam congratulated him for his admission of the failures of communism, and he suggested that the Soviet leader consider the alternative to communist ideology posed by Islam. In order to acquaint the Russian leader with Islam, Imam Khomeini recommended the works of the philosophers Farabi[11] and Ibn Sina (Avicenna),[12] and the mystic, Ibn al-

---

[10]The English rendition of the said letter of Imam Khomeini to Mikhail Gorbachev along with explanatory notes is published by this Institute under the title, A Call to Divine Unity. Its second edition is forthcoming. The same is also available in other languages. (Eds.)

[11]One of Islam's leading philosophers, al-Farabi was born at Farab, situated on the Jaxartes (Syr Darya), the modern Otrar. Coming to Baghdad, he studied under the Christian doctor Johanna, son of Hilan. Another of his teachers was Abu Bishr, Matta, known as a translator of Greek works. He next proceeded to Aleppo, to the court of Sayf ad-Dawlah, son of Hamdan, and led a somewhat retired life under his protection, assuming the garb of a Sufi. When this prince captured Damascus, he took the philosopher with him, and there Farabi died in 339 AH/950.

Farabi's literary production was considerable, but a great number of his works was lost very early. They were chiefly commentaries or explanations of the Greek philosophers, especially Aristotle. He wrote An Introduction to Logic, A Concise Logic, a series of commentaries on the Isagoge of Porphyry, the Categories, the Hermenia, the First and Second Analytics, the Topics, Sophistic, Rhetoric, and Poetics. The whole formed an Organon divided into nine parts. In the sphere of Moral Philosophy he wrote a commentary on the Nicomachean Ethics; in that of political philosophy, he made a summary of Plato's Laws, and composed a short treatise on the Ideal City. To psychology and metaphysics he contributed numerous works, with such titles as Intelligence and the Intelligible, The Soul, The Faculties of the Soul, The One and Unity, Substance, Time, The Void, and Space and Measure. He also commented on Alexander of Aphrodisias' book, de Anima. Believing that Greek philosophy was a unity, he labored to reconcile Plato and Aristotle, and with this idea wrote treatises on The Aims of Plato and Aristotle and The Agreement between Plato and Aristotle. He also discussed certain interpretations of Aristotle proposed by Galen and John Philoponus, and composed An Intervention between Aristotle and Galen.

In the sphere of science, Farabi wrote commentaries on Aristotle's Physics, Meteorology, The Heavens, and The Universe, besides commenting on the Almagest of Ptolemy. To him also is due an essay explaining some difficult propositions from the Elements of Euclid. The occult sciences interested him, and he left writings on alchemy, geomancy, genii, and dreams.

This great philosopher was also a talented musician, a somewhat exceptional combination. In this sphere he was at the same time composer, virtuoso, and theorist. (Pub.)

[12]Abu 'Ali al-Husayn ibn 'Abdullah ibn Sina, or Avicenna, entitled *al-Shaykh al-Ra'is*, or *Hujjat al-Haqq* by his compatriots, simply Shaykh by his disciples, and the Prince of Physicians in the occidental world, was born near Bukhara in the year 370 AH/980. When Ibn Sina was five years old he and his family moved to the city of Bukhara, where the young boy had a greater opportunity to study. At the age of ten he already knew grammar, literature, and theology as well as the whole of the Qur'an. When the famous mathematician, Abu 'Abdullah al-Natili, came to Bukhara, he was invited to stay at the house of Ibn Sina in order to teach him mathematics. Under his tutelage Ibn Sina mastered the Almagest, the Elements of Euclid and some logic, all of which he soon knew better than his teacher. Having mastered mathematics, he then turned his attention to physics, metaphysics, and medicine. By the time he was sixteen Ibn Sina had mastered all the sciences of his day and was well known as a physician. In another two years, thanks to the commentary of al-Farabi, he was also to complete his understanding of Aristotle's metaphysics which at first had presented considerable difficulty for him.

Despite the loss in part or in toto of several of his major works, such as the twenty-volume *Kitab al-Insaf* on the arbitration of Eastern and Western philosophy and the *Lisan al-'Arab* in ten volumes, over two-hundred and fifty books, treatises, and letters of Ibn Sina have survived. They

'Arabi. Conservative clerics were incensed that Imam should choose to represent Islamic thought through the works of philosophers and a Sufi, instead of works of jurisprudence and traditional devotional literature. President Gorbachev politely declined the invitation to convert, although he said that he would consider the importance of spiritual values in society. Imam Khomeini appears to have been genuinely disappointed that the response was not affirmative, and when a Soviet delegate read Gorbachev's reply to Imam Khomeini in Tehran, Imam repeatedly interrupted with criticism of the views expressed in the letter. Such unconventional diplomacy demonstrates Imam's propagation, despite criticism from the clergy which he championed. It also provides an indication of the unusual way in which mysticism and politics were combined in the thinking of Imam Khomeini.

---

range from the voluminous *Kitab ash-Shifa* and al-*Qanunfi't-Tibb* to treatises of only a few pages like *Risalat al-Fi'lwal-Infi'al* and *Risalahfi's-Sirr al-Qadar*.

His books can be roughly divided into four separate groups: the philosophical, religious, cosmological and physical, and finally the symbolical and metaphysical narratives.

Kitab ash-Shifa, a vast philosophical and scientific encyclopedia, is probably the largest work of its kind ever written by one man. *Al-Qanunfi't-Tibb* is the most famous single book in the history of medicine in both the East and West. In the West, this book became the only medical authority for several centuries and Ibn Sina enjoyed an undisputed place of honor. In the East his dominating influence in medicine, philosophy and theology has lasted over the ages and is still alive within the circles of Islamic thought. (Pub.)

Imam wrote several works which treated mystical topics, or which treated topics in a way characteristic of the mystical tradition. Their titles are suggestive: *Commentary on the Supplication before Dawn (Sharh ad-Du'a as-Sahar), The Lamp of Guidance to Vicegerency and Guardianship (Misbah al-Hidayat ala'l-Khilafat wal-Wilayah), The Countenance of Allah (Liqa' Allah), The Secret of Prayer: Prayers of the Gnostics or Ascension of the Wayfarers (Sirr as-Salat: Salat al-'Arifin ya Mi'raj as-Salikin), Annotation to the Commentary on 'The Bezels of Wisdom' (Ta'liqatala Sharh al-Fusus al-Hikam), Annotation to the Commentary on 'The Lamp of Intimacy' (Ta'liqatala Sharh al-Misbah al-Uns),* two books of commentaries and annotations to another commentary on a collection of reports regarding the Prophet and Imams called Ras al-Jalut, Lectures on *Surah al-Fatihah, Marginalia to 'The Journeys' (Hashiyeh ala'l-Asfar), The Disciplines of the Prayer (Adab as-Salat),*[13] *Commentary on Forty Sayings of the Prophet and Imams (Chehel Hadith).*[14]

After he became a *marja'-e taqlid*, political events dominated the life of Imam Khomeini. In 1963, the Shah's forces massacred thousands who protested against the

---

[13]Imam Khomeini, *Adab as-Salat*: The Disciplines of the Prayer, 2nd ed. (Tehran: The Institute for Compilation and Publication of Imam Khomeini's Works, 2002). (Eds.)

[14]Imam Khomeini, Forty Hadiths: An Exposition of Ethical and Gnostic Traditions, tr. 'Ali Quli Qara'i (Tehran: The Institute for Compilation and Publication of Imam Khomeini's Works, 2003). (Eds.)

dictatorship. Imam Khomeini was arrested for his inflammatory speeches and was taken to Tehran. Later he was released with the announcement that he had agreed to refrain from further political activity. He denied that he had made any such agreement and was picked up again. He was taken to an unknown destination by car. When the car turned off the main highway, it is reported that Imam imagined that he would be assassinated in a remote quarter of the desert. He felt his heart to see if it was racing, but found out that it was calm. He narrated that he was never afraid. He was taken to a small airstrip where a plane waited to take him to exile in Turkey.

The following year his place of exile was changed to the shrine city of Najaf in southern Iraq. Imam Khomeini remained in Najaf for fourteen years, and it was during these years that the lectures collected under the title, *Jihad al-Akbar* were delivered. In 1978, the Shah put pressure on the Ba'athist government in Iraq to expel Ayatullah Khomeini. After being refused asylum at the airport in Kuwait, Imam commented that he would spend his life traveling from one airport to another, but that he would not be keep silence. Finally, he was admitted to France, where he resided at Neauphle-le-Châteaux, outside Paris. In February 1979, he returned triumphantly to Iran and the Islamic Republic was launched.

A brief chronology of the political events subsequent to the victory of the Revolution is provided below, with special emphasis on the events which took place during the period in which the poetry included in this volume was written.

September 22, 1980 - Iraqi forces invaded the territory of the newly created Islamic Republic of Iran, initiating the Iran-Iraq War which would last eight years and claim hundreds of thousands of victims on both sides.

October 23, 1984 - 241 American marines were killed by a car bomb in Beirut.

March 1, 1984 - The tanker war started in the Persian Gulf. Iraqi forces were driven from the Majnun marshes and oil field.

March 4, 1985 - The War of the Cities began when Iraq launched a missile attack to Ahwaz.

July 14, 1985 - Iran announced that ships would be subject to search if they entered the Persian Gulf in order to reduce weapons supplies to Iraq.

February 10, 1986 - Iran captured Fav peninsula.

November 3, 1986 - The Iran-Contra scandal was first reported.

May 17, 1987 - 37 Americans on board the Stark were killed by an Iraqi Exocet missile.

May 19, 1987 - The US government announced that it would reflag Kuwaiti tankers.

July 31, 1987 - More than 400 pilgrims, mostly from Iran, were brutally gunned down in Mecca by Saudi security forces.

March 28, 1988 - Iraq used chemical weapons to massacre the residents of the Kurdish town in Halabja.

April 18, 1988 - Iranian forces withdrew from Fav peninsula.

June 25, 1988 - Iraq captured the Majnun marshes.

July 3, 1988 - *The Vincennes* shot down an Iranian airbus killing all 290 on board.

July 18, 1988 - Iran accepts UN resolution 598 calling for a cease-fire. Imam Khomeini commented that accepting the resolution was like taking poison, but that it was done for the good of the country.

February 14, 1989 - Imam Khomeini issued a decree calling for the execution of Salman Rushdie.

June 4, 1989 - Imam Khomeini passed away, may he rest in peace.

Of course, there were many other important events, tragedies of the war, diplomatic initiatives, etc. The chronology given above is merely a reminder of the turbulence of the events which were taking place as Imam Khomeini composed his mystical poetry. The poetry was written in a notebook given to Imam by his daughter-in-law, and on odd scraps of paper, even bits of newspaper. At one point, members of Imam's family contacted those responsible for the protection of Iran's cultural heritage to discuss how the poems could best be preserved.

It was explained that due to the acid in the scraps of paper on which Imam was writing, those papers would turn to dust in several decades. It was suggested that some special paper be purchased which could be placed where Imam could conveniently use it for his poems. Members of Imam's family suggested that something would have to be already printed on that paper because Imam did not consider his poetry fit material for a blank page, and would only write on scrap paper!

Such was the character which won the hearts of his followers. Imam Khomeini was revered for the simplicity of his lifestyle and for his rigorous attention to even supererogatory details of Islamic ritual. He is said to have always faced Mecca when he performed ablutions. He preferred to purchase the less expensive shoes. If he drank half a glass of water, he would put a piece of paper over it to keep the dust out and save the rest for later.

Some claim that he had a special relation with the twelfth Imam, the Mahdi, peace be upon him, the awaited one who will defeat injustice prior to the final judgment. Such claims are also part of the mystical tradition of Shi'ite Islam.

As soon as I started translating the poems, I realized that I had come across an invaluable resource for anyone who wanted to understand Iran, the Islamic Revolution, contemporary Islamic mysticism, or Imam Khomeini. The union between poetry and mysticism in Iranian culture is illustrious. Hafiz, Rumi and others are still recited by those who participated in the mystical tradition of Islam in Iran. Often the recitation is melodious and passionate. The themes are repeated, again and again, of the quest of the lover for the beloved, intoxication with mystical experience, the dissolution of the self through union. Almost every Iranian home contains a copy of the Qur'an and the Divan of Hafiz.

Even among the nonreligious intellectuals, poetry is a controversial topic in a way which has ceased to provoke public debate in America. New poetry, as contemporary free verse is called, has proponents and detractors. The advocates of new poetry find Hafiz stale. They don't want to hear any more poems with images of the nightingale and the cup-bearer. Imam Khomeini's poetry is expressly not modern. It is written with the imagery and cadences of Hafiz. Some dismiss this poetry as amateurish, simply an imitation of Hafiz. However, even those who would prefer new poetry will admit to the success of at least some of these poems.

If they imitate Hafiz, they do so deliberately, and in such a manner that the similarities and differences add another dimension of nuance to the poems. Scholars may puzzle over the shades of difference between the relation of the lover to the beloved as expressed in Hafiz and as depicted in the poetry of Imam Khomeini. There is also a paradoxically essential modernity in the very rejection of the modern. Of course, a great portion of the interest Imam's poetry generates is due to the window it opens on the character of Imam himself. His poetry has led to a small scale revival of the writing of poetry in the old style. It is as if the sonnet should come back into poetic fashion in contemporary England.

This aspect of Imam's poetry, the interplay between cliché, the variation on tradition, and the complexity of the mystical sentiment, is mostly lost in translation. Maybe the mere reminder of its presence in the Persian will allow readers to sense some of it in the English. It would help to be familiar with Hafiz, and the entire mystical tradition of the Shi'ite Islam. Perhaps these poems, by a man so hated by his enemies and so loved by his supporters, in Iran and abroad, can serve as an introduction to the tradition in which he participates.

The role Imam plays in his tradition is ambiguous. He has been criticized by conservatives for his departures from tradition, while Western detractors have deplored the rigidity of his 'fundamentalism.' The question of the role of women in Islamic society provides a good example of this. Imam enjoined a dress code according to which women may not appear in public without a head scarf. To Westernized women, this seems a repressive measure, but for most religious women, especially among the lower classes, the scarf was already their habit; the requirement posed no inconvenience for them.

Conservative traditionalists, on the other hand, bristled when Imam encouraged women to demand marriage contracts in which it would be explicitly stated that the woman would have the right to obtain a divorce if her husband misbehaved.[15] Westernized women would find nothing remarkable in the suggestion, because Western family law automatically provides women with the right to initiate divorce proceedings. For religious Muslim women, however, the suggestion is significant because it shows women how to

---

[15]Cf. Imam's 'Address to a Group of Women in Qum' (March 6, 1979) in Islam and Revolution, p. 264.

obtain the right available to them within Islamic law in a tradition in which the availability of this right had been too often ignored. In this way, Imam emerges as a defender of orthodoxy against excessive liberalism, and at the same time, as a reformer.

Likewise, Imam's poetry seems anachronistic from the viewpoint of the enthusiasts of non-religious new poetry. But from the perspective of the religious tradition of the clergy, Imam's use of the imagery of wine drinking and love making is shocking. The imagery itself is not so appalling, for it is the familiar language of Hafiz. What is astonishing is the use of this imagery by an Ayatullah. As one studies the life and thought of Imam Khomeini, the ambiguity of his position is reflected again and again in the mirrors of Islamic and modern culture, shards of which shine prominently in contemporary Iranian society.

Since Imam passed away, many of those who had been critical of him during his life have developed a deeper respect for him. He is revered as the father of the Revolution, and as a reformer who helped to show the relevance of Islam to the problem of modern society. His poetry also won new affection for Imam because his continued personal involvement in the mystical tradition, a tradition which continues to excite the Iranian imagination, as well as tradition which has influenced Western culture through the likes of Goethe and Emerson, and whose influence continues to unfold in work by such diverse figures as the scholar, Henri Corbin and the poet, Coleman Barks.[16]

What follows this introduction is a translation of *Badeh-ye 'Ishq*, (The Wine of Love). This is the first volume of Imam's poetry which was compiled by the Institute for the Compilation and Publication of Imam Khomeini's Works, and released in February 1990, during the eleventh anniversary of the Islamic Revolution celebrations. Two hundred thousand copies were printed. Since then, two other volumes of poems have been published as well as a volume of letters in which gnostic themes are elucidated. There are other poems and letters which remain unpublished. The nature and quantity of this material is a secret.[17]

I translated a couple of poems with the help of friends. I translated them into free verse, into rhyme, and even into song. I tried various rhyme schemes. Some versions were far from what Imam wrote both in form and substance, but they

---

[16]Henri Cobin was Professor of Islamic Religion at the Sorbonne and the editor, translator and interpreter of numerous works in mystical tradition of Iran. Coleman Barks, a poet and Associate Professor of English at the University of Georgia in Athens, has produced several remarkable volumes of American spiritual free-verse renditions of the poetry of Mawlawi Jalal ad-Din ar-Rumi.

[17]So far, a compendium of Imam Khomeini's poems has already been published. See Divan-e Imam (Tehran: The Institute for Compilation and Publication of Imam Khomeini's Works). (Eds.)

were meditations on the phenomenon of this poetry itself. I showed some of this work to the head of the Iranian Academy of Philosophy, Dr. Ghulam-Rida A'wani, and he agreed to help me to translate the entire volume of *Badeh-ye 'Ishq*. Even this title was not a straightforward matter to translate. *Badeh* can mean wine, or it can be used for other alcoholic beverages as well, like the English 'spirits,' although sometimes it is used to mean a chalice, rather than, or along with, its contents.

In English, the word chalice has strong ecclesiastic connotation which are foreign to the Islamic tradition, and the ambiguity of 'spirit' would force a pun foreign to the original. At each point of the translation, I was faced with decisions about which connotations to preserve and which to abandon. The metaphor of wine for love is a standard among Muslim mystics, and the phrase *badeh-ye 'ishq* immediately calls this metaphor to the Persian speaker's mind: The Wine of Love. This title is not Imam's. He didn't prepare his poetry for publication. This was the task of the foundation for the preservation and publication of his works. Nevertheless, problems with the title may serve as a reminder of the infamous impossibility of translating poetry. The problem is difficult enough when translating from one European language to another, where there is shared store of symbols, but the difficulty is compounded by the cultural differences between the Islamic Republic of Iran and the USA. The clichés of one culture may be novelties in another.

Badeh-ye 'Ishq comprises three sections. First, there are two letters: one by his daughter-in-law, Fatimah Tabataba'i to Imam, written as an introduction to this collection of poems a few months after Imam passed away, followed by a letter of Imam written to his daughter-in-law. Second, there are thirty-one[18] poems in *ghazal* form. Finally, there are forty-one quatrains (*ruba'iyat*), many of which were composed by Imam as acrostics on the diminutive form of his daughter-in-law's name, Fati.[19]

The process of translation was drawn out over a period of several months, during which I would come to Dr. A'wani's office, usually more than once a week with a tape recorder. Dr. A'wani would read a poem in Farsi and then explain the meanings of almost every other word. He also pointed out allusions to *hadith* and to the poetry of Hafiz, or made more general observations prompted by a line or the use of idiom. Afterward, I would listen to the cassette, interrupted by consultation with various dictionaries, and I then jotted down as close to a literal translation as I could approximate.

Then I would play with the poem, versifying it, trying different meters and styles. I often showed the work in progress to other friends, and I made more alterations. In the end, I decided to abandon all hope of capturing any of the

---

[18]That is, originally twenty-three poems plus eight from the *Sabu-ye 'Ishq* (The Jug of Love). (Eds.)

[19]Fati is the nickname of his daughter-in-law, Fatimah Tabataba'i. (Eds.)

music of Imam's poetry, much of which is quite lyrical, and to replace it by whatever seemed most natural in a free verse which would keep as close as I could manage to the literal content of Imam's poems.

My work with Dr. A'wani was completed the day before the second anniversary of the death of Imam, June 4, 1991. By the end of the following month, the American-English versions were completed, although I never have ceased to find room for improvement, and the process of revisions continued throughout the summer of 1991, during which I annotated the poems at my parents' home in New York.

The annotations, the translations, and other comments represent merely one perspective on the poet and his work. It is perspective which remains limited by ignorance and by idiosyncrasy despite the patient help I have received from Dr. A'wani, and despite the suggestions and moral support of Mahdi Hujjat, Farhad Imam, Farshad Malik-Ahmadi, Dr. Zia Muwahhid, Shahrum Pazuki, Mahdi Shaykhzadeh, and to Dr. Kamal Kharrazi and the staff of the permanent mission of Iran to the United Nations. I am grateful to them all.

It is my pleasure to offer special words of thanks to Dr. Burujerdi, the director of the Institute for Research and Study of Culture of Iran under whose auspices the Iranian Academy of Philosophy operates, who graciously invited me to become a fellow at the Academy and who has continued to be a source of encouragement. Finally, I would like to express my gratitude to my parents for their support and sympathy.

I apologize to Imam, to his family, and especially to Lady Fatimah Tabataba'i, and to all the devotees of Imam for the shortcomings of these American renditions of Imam's poetry.

Dr. Muhammad G. Legenhausen
September 16, 1991
Shahrivar 25, 1370 AHS
Rabi' al-Awwal 6, 1412 AH

THE WINE OF LOVE

Mystical poetry of Imam Khomeini

- Letters

  - Fatimah Tabataba'i's Letter to Imam Khomeini

  - Imam Khomeini's Reply to Fatimah Tabataba'i

- *Ghazal* Poetry

- *Ruba'iyat* (Quatrains) Poetry

■ Letters

In the Name of Allah, the Compassionate, the Merciful

> *The fragrance of union with you*
> *has ignited these sparks within me;*
> *But grief in my breast for you*
> *has extinguished their flaring in me.*
> *What a sign to the worlds are you,*
> *worlds resounding so mournfully,*
> *With cries to whom all praise is due,*
> *extolling His endless Glory!*[1]

My dear Imam, my revered guide!

Those responsible for the publication of your works have asked me to write what I know about the manner in which you composed your mystic[2] poetry, so that a small window could thereby be opened upon this dimension of your existence for the eyes of your devotees. But when I pick up the pen, the sorrow of your loss keeps me from writing, and grief over your departures does not release me. Alas, without you, our house has no light or radiance. Every place in the house bears some

---

[1] Below is a more literal rendering of the same poem by Fatimah Tabataba'i'. Its four lines are in *ghazal* form, with first, second and fourth lines rhyming. The first line is in Arabic. Verse which mixes Arabic and Farsi is highly renowned.

"The fragrance of union with you has ignited sparks of passion for you within me. Grief for you in my breast has kept the small fire from flaring, as you wished. What a sign you are to the worlds which are filled with the sound of the wailing of the holy, Which passes the apex of the beyond: Hail to the eternal Glory, hail!"

[2] *Irfani* is the adjectival form of '*irfan*, a kind of mysticism or gnosis which flourishes in the context of Shi'i Islam.

3

token of you. The perfume of your presence is everywhere. Your little 'Ali[3] is constantly looking for you and asking about you. Since we told him that you are in heaven, in his eagerness to see you he keeps on gazing toward the sky and the stars.

No more than three months have elapsed since your spiritual journey. Every day your devotees gather at the *Husayniyyah*[4] and at your house and weep like bereaved lovers. They strew petals in the passageway between the house and the *Husayniyyah*.

My *pir*![5] You were aware of your lover's state: you knew about my enamored soul, and you knew how enthralled by you and how agitated I am, so how could you leave me alone? How can I, who have spent my entire life in the shining rays of your existence, now live in darkness?!

In this, my black night, I've lost the way to my intended.
Come out from some corner, oh star of guidance![6]

I will leave an account of this sore grief and anguish for another opportunity, and confine myself to what has been requested of me, because:

The stories of the gnostic masters nourish the soul.
Go, ask of the mystery; then come, and tell us the tale.[7]

---

[3]'Ali is the son of Sayyid Ahmad, who is the son of Imam. 'Ali's mother is the author of this letter, Fatimah Tabataba'i.

[4]A *Husayniyyah* is a place for the remembrance of the third Imam, the grandson of the Prophet, Husayn, peace be with him. The *Husayniyyah* mentioned here is the place where Imam delivered his speeches, attached to his house in northern Tehran.

[5]*Pir* literally means old man, but it is also used as spiritual title, especially among mystics, for one's spiritual master.

[6]This couplet is from Hafiz.

4

When I was reading philosophical texts required for my field of study, I would occasionally bring some of the difficult and obscure passages of a book before Imam (may his grave be hallowed) for consultation. These question and answer periods were soon transformed into twenty minute lessons. One morning when I went to him to begin a lesson, I discovered that he had written me a warning in a satirical quatrain:

> *Fati, who studies the branches of philosophy,*
> *Knows only 'ph', 'l', and 's' of philosophy,*[8]
> *My hope is that in the light of God*
> *She may unveil herself of philosophy!*

After receiving this quatrain, I very persistently began to request other verses. A few days later:

> *Fati, one must journey to the Friend,*
> *The self of one's own self one must transcend!*
> *Bits of knowledge that toward yourself tend*
> *Are devils to avoid in the way you wend.*[9]

Little by little, my insistent pleas had their effect, for a little later he composed this:

---

[7] This is another couplet from Hafiz.

[8] In Arabic, these letters spell *fals*, a small coin, or farthing.

[9] More literally:

Fati, one must journey toward the Friend,

One must pass beyond the self of one's self.

Everything known which has the scent of your being,

Is a devil in the way which you must avoid.

5

Fati, you and the Reality of gnosis.
what does it mean?!
To apprehend the essence without attributes,
what does it mean?!
Without study of 'A', you shall not find your way to 'Z'.
Without having entered the spiritual path, being gifted
what does it mean?!

I listened with my entire soul to such succinctly expressed quatrains of enlightening advice. I hung them like pendants from my ears and became intoxicated by their sweetness. Suddenly, I came to realize that it would be a pity for message about gnosis such as these to be kept private. Therefore, I boldly persisted in my request that he not abandon the line he had taken up with composition of these massages. I must confess that I was encouraged to persevere by the boundless kindness of that dear, and so, I augmented my pleas with a request for *ghazal.*[10] He reproached me, saying, "What, am I a poet?!" But as before, I insistently persisted with my spiritual guide, and after a few days I heard this:

In so far as the Friend is, you will not be harmed.
In so far as He is, the dust of quality and quantity is naught
Abandon whatever there is, and choose Him.
There is no more excellent advice than these two words.[11]

****

You have not become a lover if you have a name.

---

[10]The *ghazal* is a lyric form of Persian poetry, with rhyme in the first two and in even numbered lines, and allowing various metric forms. With respect to content, it usually does not express the linear development of an idea, but rather its couplets express variations on an idea or mood.

[11]The 'two words' are 'abandon' and 'choose,' which reflect the negative and positive elements in the first article of Muslim faith: There is no god but God.

6

You are not a mad if you have a message.
You have not become drunk if you have consciousness.
Be considerate with us until you have the goblet.

Days passed and every once in a while Imam paid the price of my ardent entreaties with a *ghazal* or with some writings. With this turn of events, I would allow no further delay, and I first showed the collection of quatrains to my spouse, Ahmad.[12] He also expressed his enthusiasm and encouraged me to pursue the case. So, I took a notebook to Imam and I requested that when suitable he inscribe therein his poems, admonitions, and mystical allusions... And it was in this way that he so graciously complied with my request and granted me a position from the table of his gnosis and generosity as provision for my journey, and he gave me something he had written which ended with a *ghazal*. It was a positive answer to my persistent request.

Now, the fruit of these efforts, that is, this valuable legacy, I place at the disposal of that respectable institute which publishes his works so that they may present it to the devotees of Imam, and thereby to provide the limpid water of this fountain for those who thirst. In this context I have other things to say which, if God grants me the opportunity, I shall relate.

In grief, untimely days elapsed;
Days accompanied by inner burning,
If the days have gone, let them go without fear,
But you stay, like unto whom there is no purity.[13]

Fatimah Tabataba'i
23/6/1368 AHS
(Sept. 12, 1989)[14]

---

[12]It refers to the son of Imam, Hujjat al-Islam wal-Muslimin Haj Sayyid Ahmad Khomeini. (Eds.)
[13]From Mawlawi Jalal ad-Din ar-Rumi.

[14]Iranians use three calendars: the lunar Islamic calendar is used for religious occasions and is indicated by AHL/AH; for national events the Persian solar calendar is used, AHS; Gregorian calendar dates are indicated by C.E. Approximate Christian era dates will be given in brackets below dates on other calendars.

8

In the Name of Allah, the Compassionate, the Merciful

My Dear Fati,

It seems that you have finally succeeded in your imposition on me to write a few lines, disregarding my excuses: old age, infirmity, and a full schedule. Now I will begin my speech with the blight of old age and of youth, both of which have afflicted me, or you could say, the ends of which I have reached. Now, inclining towards the *barzakh*,[15] if not toward hell, I am wrestling with the minions of the angel of death. Tomorrow, the black letter of my deeds shall be handed to me, and I shall be asked for an account of my misspent life. I have no answer, except my hope in the mercy of He Whose mercy embraces all things,[16] He who revealed to the Mercy of Worlds:[17] "do not despair of the mercy of Allah; surely Allah forgives sins."[18] I take it that I am to be included among those to whom these *ayat*[19] must be applied. But as for the ascension to the sacred premises of His greatness, and mounting to the neighborhood of the Friend, and joining in the banquet of Allah, to which one must arrive by means of the steps he himself has taken, how can it be? In my youth, when I had vigor and ability, die to the

---

[15]The *barzakh*, literally means an isthmus, is the interval between the death of the individual and the general resurrection. It is mentioned in the Qur'an, (23:100): "And after them shall be a *barzakh* until the day they shall be raised."

[16]This refers to what God says in the Qur'an, (7:156): "My mercy embraces all things."

[17]This is the title of the Prophet Muhammad (peace and blessings of Allah to him and to his progeny) which derives from the Qur'an, (21:107), "And We did not send you but as a mercy to the worlds."

[18]Qur'an 39:53.

[19]The chapters of the Qur'an are divided into *ayat*, which do not always correspond to what would be considered verses.

9

machinations of Satan and his minion, the commanding self[20] I became preoccupied with various notions and grandiose expressions by which I acquired neither concentration nor a spiritual state, because I never took in the spirit of these things. I didn't go from the exoteric to the esoteric, from the earthly domain to the angelic domain. I finally realized that I did not gain anything from all the clamor of the casuistry of the seminary but some heart-rending words. I was sunk so deeply among such expressions and such regards that instead of seeking to lift the veils, I collected books as if nothing else mattered in the entire world but a handful of papers. In the name of the humanities, divine goals and philosophical truth, the seeker, who has been endowed with a divine nature, is diverted and sinks beneath a great veil. The weighty tomes of *The Four Journeys*[21] diverted me from my journey to the Friend; I acquired no opening from *The Openings*,[22] nor any wisdom from The Bezels of *Wisdom*,[23] let alone from other books, for each of which is another sad story. When I reached old age, with every step, I was gradually drawn away[24] from that misfortune, until I reached senility, and what is beyond senility, with which I am now wrestling. "And among you are some who are brought back to a most decrepit life, so that they do not

---

[20]The *nafs al-ammarah*, the commanding self, is mentioned in the Qur'an, (12:53). In *'irfan*, the way of the Muslim gnostic, it is the base self, to be contrasted with the *nafs al-lawwamah*, the reproving self, (75:2), and finally, with the *nafs al-mutma'innah*, the tranquil soul (89:27).

[21]The *Asfar al-'Arba'* is the magnum opus of Sadr ad-Din Shirazi (979-1050 AH / 1571-1640), the most important Muslim philosopher since the thirteenth century.

[22]The *Futuhat al-Makkiyyah* of the great sufi theoretician, Ibn al-'Arabi (560-638 AH / 1165-1240), is an encyclopedic work projected to fill 17,000 pages in its critical edition.

[23]The *Fusus al-Hikam* of Ibn al-'Arabi, cf. fn. 1 of the introduction.

[24]This is an allusion to an expression in the Qur'an: "We will draw them on gradually whence they know not." (17:182; 68:44).

know anything after they had known.[25] You, my daughter, are miles away from this stage. You have not savored its flavor. May God extend your life to such an age, but without its ill effects. You expect writings and discourses from me, and that in the form of a mixture of poetry and prose! You don't seem to realize that I am neither a writer nor a poet nor an orator. You, my dear daughter, without having reached the stage of unripe grapes, wish to attain the stage of confection made from boiled ripe grapes! Know that a day shall come when, God forbid, you will bear the heavy burden of regret upon your shoulders for having misspent your youth with such infatuations while you let the higher things escape you, just as I have, I who have fallen behind in the caravan of lovers. So, listen to this wretched who bears such a burden on his shoulders, and who is bent beneath it. Don't be satisfied with expressions such as these, which are a trap of the great Beelzebub.[26] Seek the Great and Glorious One! Youth with its delights and gratifications are soon past. I've been through it all, through all these, and now I'm wrestling with the chastisement of hell. The Satan within does not let up on me. May Almighty God forbid that he should strike the last blow. But despair of the embracing mercy of the Divine is itself a grievous enormity. May God protect the sinner from such an affliction. It is said that at the end of his life, Hajjaj ibn Yusuf[27] that great murderer of history, said, "Oh God! Forgive me, even though I know that everyone says You will not forgive me!"

---

[25]From the Qur'an: 16:70 and 22:5.

[26]The Qur'anic name of the devil is used here, Iblis.

[27]Hajjaj ibn Yusuf (d. 714 C.E.) was a lieutenant appointed by the Umayyad caliph, 'Abd al-Malik (r. 685-705 C.E.). In order to suppress dissent in Mecca, he ordered the bombardment of the sacred mosque. He is famous for his bloody persecution of the Shi'ites, particularly for having killed Sa'id ibn Jubayr (d. 713 C.E.), who was one of the early exegetes of the Qur'an. It is reported that Hajjaj was tormented by the image of this martyr in his dying moments.

Upon hearing of this, Shafi'i[28] said, "If he has said this, it may be (that he is forgiven)." But I don't know whether that wicked man was blessed to say this or not, but I know that despair is worse than anything. Oh my daughter, don't be so overconfident of mercy that you neglect the Friend, nor should you despair and thus become one of those who has lost both this world and the hereafter. Oh God! By the five companions of the cloak,[29] shelter Ahmad, Fati, Hasan, Rida (Yasir) and 'Ali, who, we are proud to say, belong to the household of your dear Prophet, and to the household of his appointed one.[30] Shelter them from the evils of Satan and from the desires of the soul. Here ends my speech, and God's sentence upon me is complete. Peace!

Since you have demanded poems from me with that insistence which is so characteristic of you, I must confess that neither in my youth, which is the season of poetry and sensitivity, and which has now been spent, nor in the season of old age, which I have also left behind me, nor in this most decrepit state of life, with which I am now wrestling, have I ever had a talent for poetry. It is related that someone said, "My power is no different in old age from what it was in my youth, for I have remained unable to lift this stone both in youth and in old age." I could say the same thing about poetry and literature,

---

[28]Shafi'i (d. 820 C.E.) was the founder of one of the four schools of Sunni jurisprudence.

[29]It is reported that on a day known as *Mubahilah*, the Prophet Muhammad (peace and blessings of Allah be upon him and his progeny) gathered 'Ali, Fatimah, Hasan, and Husayn under his mantle and said, "Oh Lord, these are the people of my household." Imam uses the occasion of praying for the five members of his daughter-in-law's family as a reminder of the family of the Prophet.

[30]Imam Khomeini prays for the five members of the family of his daughter-in-law, and mentions that they are descendants of the Prophet (peace and blessings of Allah to him and his progeny) through his appointed successor, 'Ali.

for I have remained incapable of them through both my youth and old age. Thus I declare:

If 'poet' be the word for Sa'di of Shiraz,[31]
What you and I may weave is but a play of dross.[32]

Now, since I'm incapable of poetry, I'll play a trick[33] with doggerel, and so concede to your demands.

Ahmad is from Muhammad the chosen one
    Whom the Praised One shall watch from above.[34]
Fati is from the throne of the womb of Fatimah
    Whom the Creator of the heavens shall love.
Hasan, a fruit of this tree of beauty,

---

[31] Shaykh Muslih ad-Din Sa'di (1184-1283) was one of the greatest Persian poets. Born in Shiraz, he studied Sufi mysticism at the Nizamiyyah madrasah at Baghdad, with Shaykh 'Abdul-Qadir al-Jilani and with Shihab ad-Din Suhrawardi. He made the pilgrimage to Mecca many times and traveled to Central Asia, India, the Seljuq territories in Anatolia, Syria, Egypt, Arabai, Yemen, Abyssinia, and Morocco. His best known works are *Bustan* (Garden) and *Golestan* (Rose-Garden), also known as *Sa'di Nameh*. The former is a collection of poems on ethical subjects, the latter a collection of moral stories in prose. He also wrote a number of odes, and collections of poems known as Pleasantries, Jests and Obscenities. His influence on Persian, Turkish and Indian literatures has been very considerable, and his works were often translated into European languages from the 17th century onwards. (Eds.)

[32] Literally:

    If Sa'di of Shiraz is a poet,
    The weavings of you and me are play.

[33] The expression *bazidadan*, literally to give a play, is sometimes used in the sense of to deceive, cheat, or to increase the stakes of a game. Imam's usage of the term is peculiar to him.

[34] One of the names of God is al-Hamid, the Praised One. The name Ahmad, Imam Khomeini's son, the name Muhammad, and Hamid all come from the same root in Arabic. Ahmad is also used as a name of the Prophet. This sort of play on words continues through the poem. For example, Hasan and Muhsin, the Benefactor, have the same root. The children of Imam's son, Sayyid Ahmad are 'Ali, Rida (also called Yasir) and Hasan.

13

The Benefactor shall be his sure companion boon.
Yasir, of the pure house of the two offspring,[35]
 The secrets of sanctity about him shall be strewn.
'Ali who is from the garden of 'Ali,
 His slogan shall be 'Ali is great.
Five persons from the loins of Ahmad
 Shall find intercession from the four plus eight.[36]
My daughter asks me for fresh poetry,
 Doggerel, I say, as mementoes of late.

Again you ask for poetry, and yet again, so here is some more babble:

I am a lover, a lover!
 Except for union with You
  there is no cure for this,
Who is there
 whose soul has not been kindled
  by this fire?
Except for you,
 in the assembly of those burnt of heart,
  nothing is remembered.
This is a story
 with neither a beginning
  nor an end.
The mystery of the heart

---

[35]This refers to the two grandsons of the Prophet, Hasan and Husayn.
[36]The four plus eight are the twelve Imams of Shi'i Islam.

cannot be exposed
                    to anyone
Except to the Friend
          for whom there is neither presence
                    nor absence.
With whom may I confide,
          that one can never
                    see the Friend,
Unless neither thought
          nor vision
                    is under his control?
Open a corner of your eye
          to look
                    at this poor man;
Engage him with the play of love,
          for this is a disorderly wilderness.
Open the cask
          and fill the goblet to the brim.
Except for You,
          None gives the true measure
                    nor keeps its promise.[37]
The tongue cannot be stilled
          From the distracted talk
Of one in whose breast is only
          a distracted heart.
Tear up the tablet,
          break the pen,

---

[37]Here there is a pun between the words for promise, *payman*, and for measure, *paymaneh*, which indicates the cup.

and breath nothing more,

For there is no one
who is not baffled and bewildered
by Him.

Azar 1365 AHS
Rabi' ath-Thani 1407 AH
(November-December 1986)

Ghazal Poetry

The Consolation of the Pir

Kiss the hand of the shaykh *who has pronounced me a disbeliever.*

Congratulate the guard who has led me away in chains.

> *I'm going into a solitary retreat*
>
> > *from noon by the door of the Magus,*
>
> *So that in one gulp I may be filled*
>
> > *with the wine of both worlds.*
>
> *I will not drink the water of* Kawthar*;*
>
> > *I will not take this heavenly favor.*
>
> *The beam which shines on your face, oh Friend,*
>
> > *has made me a conqueror of the world.*
>
> *Console the heart of the dervish from whom the eternal secret*
>
> > *Has been disclosed; who has made me aware of my destiny.*

I congratulate the Pir of the tavern who has himself grasped

My annihilation, my nothingness, and who has captivated me,

> *A servant of my Pir, who comforts the heart himself,*
>
> *Of one who has forgotten himself and whom he has turned upside down.*

Esfand 1367 AHS
[February-March 1989]

Explanation

This kind of poem, like the next thirty[38] which follow, is a *ghazal*. Persian is a poetic language. Ordinary rhymes are easy to come by, so most poetry uses feminine rhymes which would be awkward and silly and impossibly difficult to manage in English. In Farsi, the poem has a rhyme scheme like this:

-------*iramkard*

-------*iramkard*

-------*iramkard*

------*iramkard*

------*ramkard*

------*iramkard*

The sound "*iramkard*" is a combination of the ending sound of a verb, a first-person pronoun, and an auxiliary verb, which results in the triple rhymes that runs through the poem.

Imam Khomeini's poetry is a kind of play with the images and themes of Hafiz (d.1338 CE), the undisputed master of the *ghazal*. In this poetry there is always a contrast between official hypocritical religion, represented by the mosque and the seminary, and the true religion, symbolized by the tavern, the wine, the cupbearer, the Zoroastrian priest, idols, sexual love, etc. This tension is heighten in Imam Khomeini's poetry

---

[38]That is, originally twenty-two poems plus eight from the *Sabu-ye 'Ishq* (The Jug of Love). (Eds.)

precisely because he is as official a representative of official religion as one could ever hope to find, and yet he sees himself, in his most private vision, as an iconoclast. Consider the first line: "Kiss the hand of the shaykh who has pronounced me a disbeliever." This pronouncing that someone is a disbeliever is the job of the official clergy, as Imam Khomeini in his official capacity as a jurist condemned Salman Rushdie. Perhaps it is more than a coincidence that the decree [*fatwa*] was issued right about the time that this poem was written. The title 'shaykh' is ambiguous. In contemporary Iran the term is used for masters of mysticism. In Arab countries, like Iraq, this title is still used for a jurist, an official cleric, although it is also used like the Persian *pir* for a gnostic master, or even as a common title of respect for an old man. In classical Persian poetry, particularly in the poetry of Hafiz, the shaykh symbolizes hypocritical observance of the outward forms of religion without regard for its true inner spirit. "Congratulate" occurs twice in the poem. This is not a translation of the Persian word *benevaz*. When a child performs some task well, one may stroke the face of the child and praises the child. *Benevaz* signifies that one should perform this sort of laudatory stroking. The word that I've translated as "guard" is *mohtaseb* which was the title for a certain low level government functionary, a kind of inspector, during the time of Hafiz, seven hundred years ago. So, in the very first couplet of this poem, we meet three aspects of Imam Khomeini's own personality: the cleric, the leader of government, and the mystic. The mystic is the inner self, the first person in whose voice the poem is narrated, and it is this person which is condemned as a disbeliever by the others, while the mystic accepts and appreciates the cleric and guard. This theme is repeated in the poem, as he says that in one gulp he has been filled with the wine of both worlds. He has been filled with

21

the wine of this worldly devotion as cleric and leader, and with the wine of other worldly devotion as mystic and poet. The Magus, *Pir-e Moghan*, is a Zoroastrian elder, interchangeable with the pir of the tavern, and the bar keeper. The "water of *Kawthar*" is a spring in paradise which is mentioned in the Qur'an (108:1-2).

The Wine of Love

I am a hunter of taverns, don't ask me about the Beloved.
I am dumb, so from the dumb, and distracted don't ask for an
oration.
I'm preoccupied with my own blindness and wretchedness,
So from the blind don't ask for sight and vision.
Your languid eyes have brought on my own languor,
So don't ask from one so smitten for aught but delirious ravings.
Don't consort with a wandering dervish, but if ever you do,
Never ask him about wisdom, philosophy, scripture, or of the
sayings of the Prophet.
I am drunk with the wine of Thy love, so from such a drunkard
Don't ask for the sober counsel of a man of the world.

Dey 1365 AHS
[December-January 1986/87]

Explanation

In this poem, as in the previous poem, Imam Khomeini may be playing with different facets of his own personality. He was famous for his speeches, some of which have been translated by Hamid Algar in *Islam and Revolution* (Berkeley: Mizan Press, 1981), yet in this poem he protests that he is not to be asked for an oration. He is a philosopher and theologian, yet he cautions that one should not turn to him for philosophical insight. He is a cleric who has written a famous commentary on forty sayings of the Prophet, a partial translation of which has been published as *Forty Hadiths: An Exposition of Ethical and Mystical Traditions, Part 1* (Tehran: Islamic Propagation Organization,

23

1989).[39] All of this is superceded by his inner life as a mystic lover. The language used to express this is that of Hafiz. The tavern, *kharabat*, may also be brothel or gaming house. In the tradition of Hafiz, it is the place of mystical ecstacy, where the 'wine,' the love of God, is served. The Beloved, *yar*, or friend/companion, is commonly taken to indicate God. The languid eye, *cheshm-e bimar*, literally sick eye, is used for the seductive languid eye of a mistress, and this genre of poetry is understood to mean the spiritual attraction of the divine. The 'sick eye' of the intoxicated beloved is half-closed, disdainful. The wandering dervish mentioned in the poem is a *Qalandar*, an itinerant dervish with a reputation for being something of a rogue. *Hikmat*, literally wisdom, has the technical meaning of a kind of philosophical theology or theosophy.

---

[39]The English translation of the whole book is already published by the Institute for Compilation and Publication of Imam Khomeini's Works. (Eds.)

Life's Caravan

My life has reached its end, but yet, my Friend
  has not come.
My story now concludes; but conclusion to this pain
  has not come
The goblet of death is at hand, yet I never had my turn
at the goblet of wine.
The years have come and gone, but a sweetheart's tenderness
has not come.
The bird of my spirit's been trapped, and, fallen without wings
to fly, is confined to this cage,
Yet she who should set me free, who should break apart this
cage,
has not come.[40]
The lovers of a darling face are all nameless and without
vestige
While for those of fame, even a whiff of the air of her affection
has not come.
In rank and file of the caravan of the lovers of her face,
they wait expectantly.
To whom then should I complain that at last the soul quickening
beloved has come?
She bestows the spirit of the dead, and seizes the souls of the
lovers.
To the ignorant alone, belief in such a ravishing love
has not come.

Tir 1366 AHS
[June-July 1987]

---

[40]In Farsi personal pronouns have no gender, so the use of the feminine pronouns for the beloved is somewhat arbitrary.

The Account of Perplexity

I want the pain, not the drug.
I want the anguish that sticks in the throat,
    not a pleasant melody.
I am a lover, I am a lover, I am your patient;
I don't want to be healed from this.
I would even pay for your cruelty for my soul;
I don't want to abandon this cruelty.
From you, my beloved, cruelty is fidelity,
So, I don't want any other fidelity,
You are both my Safa and my Marwa;
I don't want Marwa with Safa.
The Sufi has no news about the union with the Friend.
I don't want a Sufi without Safa.
You are my supplication and my remembrance;
I want neither remembrance nor contemplation nor supplication.
In whatever direction I turn, you are my qiblah.
I want no qiblah nor that which shows its direction.
Whoever you gaze upon becomes your sacrifice.
I am the sacrifice, I don't want any sacrifice.
Every horizon is enlightened by your visage,
You are manifest, I don't want a mere trace of you.

Ordibehesht 1366 AHS
[April-May 1987]

Explanation

This poem reminds one of the lines of Baba Tahir:

Some want the drug, some want the pain,
Some want union, some want separation,
I am not of those who want the drug, the pain, union or
separation.
I want what the beloved wants.

The idea expressed in this poem is that even in the hiddenness of God, He is manifest to the true lover. The very hiddenness itself becomes a mode of manifestation. The pain which is described in the first eight lines is the pain of the lover, the longing for union with the divine. The cruelty is the experience of this longing caused by the need for union. The word translated as 'cruelty' here, *jafa'*, indicates the kind of torment a mistress may inflict upon her lover, as by withholding her favors. The lover wants this cruelty, because he wants to feel the union with the divine. He wants no other fulfillment of any promise by God except that he should be so favored as to feel the need for union with Him. *Safa* and *Marwa* are the two hills between which pilgrims must run back and forth during the *Hajj* ceremony, to commemorate the searching of Hajar, the wife of Abraham, for water herself and for the son Isma'il. Also, it is said that when Adam and Eve were ejected from the garden, Adam was put on *Safa* and Eve on *Marwa*. So, the two hills symbolize the longing of the lovers. There is a pun in the following lines on the name *'Safa'* which means purity. In saying that the beloved is his *Safa* and *Marwa*, he claims that he has no need to perform the rites of the pilgrimage, because he already experiences the hardship of the pilgrimage in his longing for the beloved. In saying that he does not want *Marwa* with *Safa*, the lover claims both that he feels no need to perform the pilgrimage, and also that he does not want this rite with purity, that is he doesn't want to be cleansed of the hardship he

27

experiences in his longing. The sufi is one who has achieved union with the divine, yet line (11) declares that the sufi has no news of it. Line twelve (12) is ambiguous. It can mean that such a sufi, with no news of union with the divine, and thus with no purity, is not wanted, or it can mean that he does not want to be a sufi who is without the difficulty represented by Mt. Safa and alluding to the rites of the pilgrimage. Lines (13) and (14) mention *dhikr* and *fikr*, which are the chief methods employed by the sufi to attain union with the divine. *Dhikr* is the heartfelt remembrance of God, usually through the repetition of one of the names of God, or some short exclamation of praise or faith. *Fikr* is contemplation and *du'a* is a supplication. In these lines the lover states that he does not need such methods, because his yearning is sufficient. The *qiblah* is the direction of prayer towards the Ka'bah in Mecca. Lines (15) and (16) recall the *ayah* of the Qur'an:

"Withersoever you turn, there is the face of Allah"
(2:115).

In lines (17) and (18), the lover declares his devotion to the beloved with phrase, 'I am your sacrifice.' The claim, 'I want no sacrifice,' means that the lover feels no need for something to sacrifice, such as an animal, because he himself is being sacrificed to God. An animal sacrifice is part of the *Hajj* ceremony. Line (19) again recalls the above cited *ayah* of the Qur'an. In the last line, the lover declares that God is already manifest to him, and so that he neither nor wants any 'trace' (lit. footprint), any sign or symbol which could help him to find the beloved

To those unfamiliar with the tradition of Islamic mysticism, particularly as it has developed in Iran, all of this may sound somewhat shocking. However, the gesture of repudiating the outward ritual of the pilgrimage in favor of an esoteric pilgrimage of the heart can be found in the writings of a number of mystics. The rejection of the exoteric forms of religion is itself a symbol for the need to attend to the inner dimension of religion. Nevertheless, there have been members of the clergy who have opposed such symbolic repudiations of the outward forms of religion on the grounds that they may be misunderstood as authentic opposition to ritual, as the poet's verses about wine may deceive some who would seek physical instead of spiritual intoxication.

The Bright Rays of the Sun

The meadow lark sings a glad tiding:

>the season of Spring has returned.

The season for wine drinking

>and for kisses has returned .

At last the time of withering

>and melancholy has gone.

The days for a caress

>of your sweetheart's waist have returned.

At last the time of death,

>decay and ruin has gone.

Life, with two hundred images and sights

>has returned.

The meadow's wan yellow face

>has since packed up and gone.

Rosebuds in the sun's bright rays

>to blossoms have returned.

The cup-bearer, the tavern,

>the troubadour, clapping of hands,

And a fancy for the curl of a tress

>of a dear one have returned.

If you pass the gate of the seminary

>tell the shaykh

If he would be taught

the rosy cheeked girl has returned.

Close the shop of asceticism

during this season of joy,

For the strain that the tar[41] plays

has again to our ears returned.

Farvardin 1366 AHS
[March-April 1987]

---

[41]The tar is a traditional Persian stringed instrument.

Your Wine Drunk Eyes

Your wine drunk languid eyes
    Have brought on my own languor.
I've become captivated
    by your curls.
You are a cypress from the garden of excellence,
    a flower from the flower bed of beauty.
Without even an amorous glance,
    you've made me lose the interest in all
    other beauties.
All who have tasted the wine
    have lost all consciousness,
But I've become conscious
    by the goblet from your life giving hand.
What shall I do?
    I am enthralled, burning, stricken.
Your coquetry and jewel filled ruby lips
    have caused me to adore you.
My heart's love
    has brought the Mansur[42] in me

---

[42]Mansur is Mansur al-Hallaj (858-922 CE), the famous Sufi martyr made famous in the West through Louis Massignon's *magnum opus*, *The Passion of Hallaj*, tr. Herbert Mason (Princeton: Princeton University Press, 1982). Hallaj was charged with blasphemy and with claiming to have the authority to free the pious from the requirements of Islamic law. He responded to the charge of blasphemy with the explanation that when he uttered the words, "I am the Truth," he had achieved a state of mystic union with God, and was speaking not for himself, but as the instrument of God. He was whipped, mutilated, crucified, decapitated, cremated, and his remains were scattered. According to Imam Khomeini's doctrine of Absolute Guardianship of the Jurist (*wilayat al-faqihmutlaq*), the Guardian-Jurist has absolute authority, even to the point of abrogation of the laws of Islam if he deems that such measures are required for the defense of the Muslim polity. This

From my quarters
*   to ascend the scaffold.*
Your love has driven me from the seminary
*   and from the circle of the Sufis.*
And has made me the submissive slave
*   of the wine cellar.*
Wine from your brim filled goblet
*   has made me eternal.*
By kissing the dust of your threshold
*   I've become intimate with mystery.*

Dey 1365 AHS
[December-January 1986-87]

Spring at Old Age

Spring has come. I shall begin youth after old age.

I will sit beside the Friend, and have the fruit of my life.

I shall return to the rose garden. I shall mingle with the flowers and the buds.

At the side of the garden I shall caress the moon-faced sweetheart.

I shall cast behind me autumn and its yellowness one day,

For in the garden I shall get news of the rosy-cheeked dear.

My feathers and wings molt in January with agony over the sweetheart.

In April with memory of union with the darling,

I'll get wings and feathers once again.

In the time of autumn I would perch in this ruined land,

If Spring has come, it is because I am ready to take off

for the sake of union with her.

If the wine-bearer spills some wine of the goblet onto the lovers,

If she spills it out of drunkenness, I shall pull the veil from her face.

Ordibehesht 1366 AHS
[April-May 1987]

Son of the Tavern

Drink a cup at the gate of the tavern and be joyous

In remembrance of the angel who gave you this success.

Even of you do not have an adze with which to dig up the mountain

Become Farhad[43] in agony over the sweetheart and be joyous.

Go and wear the earring of servitude, of being a rogue;

Become the ruler of the world of generation and corruption.

Compose a song of the curls and waves of the tresses of the cup-bearer.

With soul and heart be the standard bearer of this custom.

Become a pupil of the master of the faculty of wine in all the branches of love.

Hold up your head over all creation and become a professor.

Drunkards do not purchase position for a farthing,

Even if they should be the Khosrow of time or Kay Qabad.

---

[43]Farhad is a romantic hero in a tale from the *Khamseh* of Nezami. Farhad is given an impossible task of digging a road through a mountain by King Khosrow who wishes to eliminate him as a rival in love. The tale is translated by Peter J. Chelkowski in the beautifully illustrated *Mirror of the Invisible World* (New York: Metropolitan Museum of Art, 1975). The single earring in a male was an indication that he was a slave. "Rogue" is used for the Persian rend, one of the most important technical terms in the poetry of Hafiz. Much has been written on the meaning of this term, and there are profound differences in interpretation. A rend is a seeker who has achieved a very high degree of spiritual excellence, to the extent that he seems somewhat of a rogue or renegade by those preoccupied exclusively with the exoteric elements of religion. Some interpreters claim that the *rend*is above religious law, while others claim that his flouting of the law is merely apparent and is purely symbolic. Khosrow, Kay Qabad, Qaysar and Kasra are all legendary kings of ancient Persian tales of whom are most widely known from Ferdowsi's *Shahnameh*.

If you become the pleasant son of the tavern,

Leave the Kingdom of Qaysar and Kasra to the winds.

15/12/67 AHS
[March 6, 1989]

The Flight of the Soul

If the way were clear to her alley before dawn,

If my sleeping fate would join me for a while,

If the morning breeze would find its way to the lane of the friend,

If my distressed heart would become intimate with that cypress stature one,

If the reed would tell of the pain of the hearts of the lovers,

If the sore heart would harmonize with the sorely desired,

If Solomon had mercy on the sorrow of a weak ant, [44]

So that it held up its head and became eminent among the companion of the heart,

In this desire I'll offer my head; for her arrival I'll shed my life,

If she opens the gate for me, and returns my affection.

Cast your shadow upon my head, O cypress of the garden of excellence,

Until my soul is ready to fly from this world.

Tir 1366 AHS
[June-July 1987]

---

[44]The reference to Solomon's mercy on the ant alludes to a passage in the Qur'an:

His host of jinn and men and birds were gathered before Solomon in ranks. When they came to the Valley of the Ants, an Ant said:

'O Ants! Go into your dwellings lest Solomon and his hosts should unwittingly crush you!

He smiled at her words, and said: O my Lord! Make me thankful for the favors You have bestowed upon me and my parents, and may I do good which will please You, and admit me, through Your mercy, among Your righteous servants." (27:17-19).

The Wine of Awakening

Take up the cup and take off the robes of asceticism and pretense,

Leave the prayer niche to the pretentious shaykh.

Inform the pir of the tavern about our state.

With a goblet he may dispel the wine craving from our souls.

The begging bowl of poverty is cause for our honor.[45]

O heart deceiving Friend, increase this honor.[46]

We eat the crumbs of the conversation of the wandering dervi rogue.

With one amorous glance, show affection to the heart of this old do eater.

Do not speak of the soul wounding poison of my rival.

Do you know what I've suffered from this speckled snake?[47]

Kisses and caresses of the Friend have given life to my soul.

In her absence I have no share of kiss nor caress.

Warn the pir of the saloon of my anguish.

The cup-bearer has made me conscious with a cup of wine.

27/11/67 AHS
[February 16, 1989]

---

[45]The begging bowl is the *kashkol*, a traditional Sufi symbol of spiritual poverty, that is, of the heartfelt need for God.

[46]This line alludes to a saying attributed to the Prophet: "Poverty is my honor."

[47]The speckled snake is infamous for its deadly poison. When Imam Khomeini accepted the ceasefire with Iraq, in September 1988, he commented that accepting UN resolution 598 was for him like taking poison.

The Miracle of Love

The Friend cried out because the secret of her was exposed.

How humiliated she was before the rogues of the saloon.

I wanted to keep the secret of my heart to myself alone.

But when the door of the bar was opened there was such a tumult!

Open the lid of the wine vat because the Friend has come!

Glad tidings O tavern, for eternal life has been established!

How I enjoy the tuft of your hair, when you undo it.

A mote becomes the sun and a drop becomes the whole sea.

You opened your lips to speak of wine and you become drunk.

Before the cup-bearer all the secrets of the world were divulged.

It is as if the Messiah has passed by the lane of the tavern,

So that at the threshold of God he should have attained such high repute.

You don't know the miracle of love. Zulaykha[48] knows it.

For with her the beloved Joseph became so beautiful.

15/12/67 AHS
[March 6, 1989]

---

[48]Zulaykha is the wife of the 'Aziz in the Qur'an, Potiphor's wife in the Bible. In the poetry of Jami, Zulaykha and Joseph marry after the death of the 'Aziz.

The Path of Nothingness

Save your love there is nothing in our hearts.

Your love was kneaded into our clay.

The Asfar and Shifa of Ibn Sina[49] did not untie

Our difficulty with all their hairsplitting disputations.

Tell the shaykh who called my way invalid,

(He will sneer at your truth, our invalidity)

If his wayfarer passes some stations,

Our station shall be path of nothingness itself.

A hundred caravans of the heart pickup to their destination,

But our negligent heart was left behind.

If Noah was saved from drowning and found his way to shore,

The drowning itself is our shore.

Khordad 1366 AHS
[May-June 1987]

---

[49]The *Asfar* is the magnum opus of MullaSadra (d. 1610 C.E.), and the *Shifa* is the major work of Avicenna, Ibn Sina (d. 1037 C.E.); both are central works of Islamic Philosophy.

40

Divulge Your Secret

The bird of the heart flutters, trying to escape this cage.

The life of the soul is exhausted, so, for a while it becomes mad.

No one knows the state of this butterfly with the burnt heart.

In the presence of the candle of the existence of the Friend, finally, what will happen?

ayfarers packed up and left these quarters;

This engorged heart has been left behind where this lane curves.

Divulge your secret, unveil your own beautiful face!

From the agony of seeing your face my eye has become like the Oxus.

O cup-bearer, remember the dry lipped ones left behind,

So your cup may be full to the brim and your drunkenness shall increase.

One day the cloud of mercy shall rain wine instead of water!

The plains shall become intoxicated and cheeks shall become rosy!

Farvardin 1366 AHS
[March-April 1987]

41

The Agony of Love

Wine from the goblet of the beloved is without consciousness.

Selflessness from the drink of this goblet is without wakening.

Your languid eye draws everyone to languor.

Forever, the sick lover has no sickness.

The lover has withdrawn his heart from everything

 save the beloved, silently,

Because he has no conversation with himself,

 save the story of love.

In whom may I confide of the sweetness

 of the pain of the agony of the beloved?

Save the agony of one occupied with love,

 the lover has no sorrow.

Pass by the sick bed, one day, of one love sick for your face;

See how he has no nurse by his sick bed,

 save for your love.

Be kind. O Friend, take the veil from your face and stop teasing.

The heart has no request of the beloved

 save for a vision.

Farvardin 1366 AHS
[March-April 1987]

The Sea and the Mirage

Release me from these countless pains,

From this rent heart and seared breast.

A lifetime has passed in anguish

   for separation from the face of the beloved

I am a bird in fire and a fish out of water.

My lot has been no mystical state,[50]

   for all this pain and life.

Old age arrived immersed in idleness

   after the prime of youth.

I did not profit from the lessons

   and discourses of the seminary.

How can one reach the sea from this mirage?

Each precept I learned, and every page I turned

Was nothing but another veil upon a veil.

Behold, O dear, in the season of your youth be conscious,

For in old age you can do nothing but sleep.

These ignoramuses who claim to have guidance

Have no gift under their Sufi robes but "I am".

Our own imperfections and defects

---

[50]The term for mystical state is hal. This is often used as a technical term of Islamic mysticism. In the mystic's spiritual development various such states will be exhibited. The Sufi robe is a patched called *kherqeh*. Imam Khomeini satirizes those who would claim to be mystics but who are still dominated by egotism. Imam Khomeini warns not only of the hypocrisy associated with symbols of exoteric religion, the mosque and seminary, but he also warns of the spiritual materialism associated with the mystics.

and the perfections and beauties of others, we

Have hidden like old age behind hair-coloring.

Breath no more of it;

tear up your notebook of vanity.

How long will you continue this vain talk

and erroneous speech?

Azar 1365 AHS
[November-December 1986]

Monastery of the Heart

Hail O cup-bearer! Cast away these sighs from the heart,[51]

So that your goblet may solve for once and for all

  the secrets of these difficulties.

With wine, block the way of the intellect

  to the monastery of the heart,[52]

For this lunatic asylum is no place for intellects.

If your heart is tied to the love of the sweetheart, leave this place,

For this tavern is naught but abode of those who have lost their hearts!

If you come to yourself for even less than a moment,

  from the intoxication of the wine,

Depart without delay from the confines of the retreat of the negligent.[53]

When you saw the color of that idol

  among the flowers of the garden of the Friend,

You separated yourself from the garden

  of the Friend by seas and shores.

You saw the way to the garden

  and to the paradise in front of you;

---

[51]This opening couplet alludes to that of a *ghazal* of Hafiz: Hail, O cup-bearer! Bring the cup for us, for whose hearts Love seemed easy at first, but proved difficult.

[52]The word translated here as 'monastery' is *khaneqah*, which signifies a Sufi meeting place, or a Sufi retreat.

[53]By 'the negligent' is meant those who have so immersed themselves in the divine that they have forgotten themselves.

You separated yourself from the way of truth

and joined yourself to the way of falsehood.

If you give your heart to the world of being

and to that which is above it,

You have tied yourself with the strand of a spider

by so many chains.[54]

28/10/67 AHS
(January 18, 1989)

---

[54]The reference to the spider's web is an allusion to an ayah from the Qur'an:

"The likeness of those who take protectors other than God is the likeness of the spider which makes a house for itself, but verily the flimsiest of houses is the house of the spider, if they but knew." (29:4).

46

Pre-Eternal Goblet

We are children of love and the adopted sons of the goblet.
By drunkenness and the sacrifice of our souls for the beloved
  we are perfected.
We have given our hearts to the tavern and to the sacrifices of
drink.
We are old servants at the threshold of the Magus.
We are bed fellows of the beloved,
  but we are being punished by separation from her.
We are drowned in union with her,
  yet in constant separation from her.
Without color or sound,[55]
  yet we are bound to color.
We are without name or address,
  yet we are always after a name.
We are war with the Sufi, the gnostic and the dervish.
We are battling with philosophy and theology.
We have fled from the seminary and from nearness to
creatures.
We are outcast by the wise and hated by the common.
Against being and against those who seek being
  we are back to back.
With nothingness, since the pre-eternal day,
  we are stride by stride.

Khordad 1366 AHS
[May-June 1987]

---

[55]The phrase 'color and sound' signifies wealth and the things of the material world; the word sound, *nawa*, by itself may have the meaning of opulence. The positive image of nothingness in the last line is most striking. In the mystical tradition, the soul must become as nothing in order to be infused with the divine, but the use of the nominalization, nothingness (*nisti*), is unusual.

The Releasing Goblet

Cup-bearer, open the gate of the tavern

Make me needless of lessons, discourses,

> *asceticism and hypocrisy.*

Place a strand of your wavy hair in my way.

Release me from scholarship, from the mosque,

> *from the lessons and from prayer.*

Like David playing a melody, bring me a goblet!

Make me forget the pain of ambition,

> *of rising and descending.*

Take away the veil

> *from the beautiful face and hair of the beloved.*

Banish me from the Ka'bah and from the kingdom of Hijaz.[56]

Fill my jug to the brim with pure wine.

With purity of heart

> *orient your heart toward that ravishing idol.*

I have been impoverished by the sorrow of separation

> *from the countenance of the beloved.*

Invite me to that goblet of wine
> *that is a universal panacea.*

28/11/67 AHS
[February 17, 1989]

---

[56]The *Ka'bah* is the House of Allah erected by the Prophet Abraham and his son, the Prophet Isma'il (peace be with them). It is the focus of the Hajj pilgrimage. The Hijaz is the part of Arabia in which Mecca is located.

That is Enough!

O you who have been rejected! Enough foolish words.

Enough repeating of repetitions.

Close the tongue of vain expressions.

Break the pen and the inkpot. Enough!

O you lover of fame! O you trickster!

Enough of your laughable tales, enough.

Your talk is for the sake of this world.

Enough tracing of meaningless words.

Leave me alone!

Enough repeating of repetitions.

Enough repeating of repetitions

Sha'ban 28, 1407 AHS
[April 27, 1987]

The Wine of Ramadan

There came the month of Ramadan[57]
The wine and the tavern died out.
The time for love and merriment and for wine
was switched to the pre-dawn hours.
The pir of the tavern and I
broke our fast with wine.
I told him that your fasting
is in days of leaves and fruits.
Make your ablution with wine
for according to the religion
of the rogues,
In the presence of the Truth,
this, your deed,
shall become fruitful.

Sha'ban 29, 1407 AHS
[April 28, 1987]

---

[57]Ramadan is the month of fasting in which Muslims refrain from all food, drink, and sexual intercourse from the first light of dawn until after sunset. Since the month of Ramadan is a month of the lunar calendar, it falls in different seasons in different years. In the year in which this poem was written, the first of Ramadan fell on April 30. The phrase 'days of leaves and fruits' refers to the May of 1987.

The Burn of Love

If the burn of love
  didn't pierce our hearts,
The King of Love
  wouldn't cast a glance toward us.
I've sold my soul
  in my desire to see the beloved.
What excuse can I give?
  I had no other commodity.
This head that went with the wind
  for the sake of union with His countenance,
If it had remained in view of the beloved,
  it would not be a head at all.
If Moses didn't see His face
  in the branches of the bush,
Without a doubt, his tree of knowledge
  would have borne no fruit.
If you carry the load of love with commitment,
  how shall you fear?
How, if the east is not in its place
  or if the west is not?
If we didn't knock on the door
  of His love Bilqis,[58]
We could not have passed

---

[58]*Bilqis* is the Queen of Sheba who became the bride of King Solomon (peace be with them).

to the court of Solomon.

Had the fowl of the garden of sanctity

reached union with Him,

Among the assembly of Your lovers

it would not be wingless and featherless.

15/12/67 AHS
[March 6, 1989]

The Confidant

Did you know that
  I am your wretched captive?
With heart and soul,
  I am the cause of your active market.
Every cruelty which was inflicted on me by you,
  I would gratefully purchase.
My God, I am your companion
  and your devotee.
A strand of your hair
  has finally lassoed me.
I am the captive of the curl of your hair,
  of a strand.
Enough, O owl,[59]
  of your talk about ruins,
For in this circle,
  I am the center of your compass.
The gnostics have cast a veil
  upon the face of the beloved.
I, the madman,
  am unveiling your face!
The lovers reveal
  your black secret.

---

[59]In Persian literature, the owl is an ominous symbol forever haunting ruins. The phrase, 'to have fallen off one's feet' is a Persian idiom used to indicate extreme weariness.

Come to me,

the intimate of your secrets.
Open your face to this old man
who has fallen off his feet.
Until the moment of death,
with all my soul, I am the lover
of the sight of you.

Esfand 9, 1367 AHS
[February 28, 1989]

The Day of Union

Don't grieve,
>> the days of separation
>>>> are coming to an end.
This craving in our heads,
>> the craving of drunkards,
>>>> is coming to an end.
She will lift
>> the curtain from
>>>> her moon like face
And glance seductively,
>> Sorrow will leave
>>>> the heart and spirit.
The nightingale will appear
>> among the stems
>>>> of the flowers.
The raven will leave
>> the garden in
>>>> hundredfold shame.
The meeting will be lit
>> by the light
>>>> of her face.
Everything but the memory of the beloved
>> will pass from the memory
>>>> of the rogues.

The clouds will disappear
before the light of the sun
of her face.
The curtain will disappear
from the face
of the sauntering cypress.
O friends, glad tidings!
The day of our appointment
is coming.
The days of separation are ending,
and the day of union
is coming.

Esfand 1367 AHS

[February-March 1989]

The Retreat of the Drunkards[60]

I did not find purity in the sessions of the dervishes.

   Within the cloister, I heard none call on Him.

I did not find the Friend in the books of the seminary.

   At the top of the minaret, I saw no sound of the Beloved.

I did not uncover anything in any scholarly books.

   In the lessons of Scripture, I was led nowhere.

I spent my life in the temple, spent my life in vain.

   Among my companions, I found neither cure nor affliction.

To the circle of the lovers I would go, and there I find

   a breeze from the garden of a sweetheart, and footprints.

The 'we' and 'I' of the intellect are a halter.

   There is neither 'I' nor 'we' in the retreat of the drunkards.

---

[60]This poem and the following seven are taken from *Sabu-ye 'Ishq* (The Jug of Love) as translated by Dr. Legenhausen and Sarvdalir. See *A Jug of Love*, op. cit., pp. 9-26. (Eds.)

The Drunkenness of the Lover

The heart not unsettled by your face is no heart at all;

The one not deranged by your mole is not reasonable.

From your cask has come the drunkenness of the heart-lost lover;

The outcome of my life is this drunkenness, no other.

The love of your face has cast me into this desert.

What can be done? There is no end to this desert.

If between you and Him, besides you stands none else.

If you are a heart-lost lover, abandon yourself.

Throw away your robe[61] and prayer mat,

if you would tread the way of love.

Because for you there is no way

in this station except for love.

If you are of those of the heart,

abandon the ascetic and Sufi,

For except for this group,

there is no way in this assembly.

I clutch the curl of her ringlet while playing,

For except for this, the outcome of this madness is nothing.

Take my hand and release me from this robe of pretense,

For in this robe there is room for nothing but ignorance.

In the tavern, learning and mysticism have no way,

For in the station of the lovers, fallacy has no way.

---

[61]The robe mentioned here is the patched robe of the Sufi, the *kherqeh*, which, though originally a symbol of poverty, came to be worn with pride by those who would feign deep spirituality. By the time of Hafiz (d. 791 AH/1389), the patched robe had become a symbol of affected spirituality, so that he would end one of his *ghazals*: "Hafiz, throw away the wooden *kherqeh* and go."

The Assembly of the Rogues [62]

The day will come when I will be dust,
  I will be dust in her alley.
I will have abandoned the soul,
  unsettled by her face.
I will take the goblet from her hand
  that increases the spirit.
I will pay heed to neither of the worlds,
  bound with her hair.
I will rest my head on her feet,
  kissing them 'till the instant of death.
I will be drunk with the wine of her jug
  'till the morning of the resurrection.
I will be a moth, burning,
  burning all my life in her candle.
I will be drunk with wine,
  marveling at her beautiful face.
The day will come when I will be drunk,
  tipsy in the assembly of the rogues.
I will be the keeper of the mysteries,

---

[62]The rogue is the Persian *rend*, one who is known for his unorthodox cleverness, and the hero of the poetry of Hafiz. The assembly is the session of the mystics, in which they gathered in a circle around the master.

of all her unspeakable secrets.

If my Joseph does not come

To comfort me in my sickbed,

Then my heart, like Jacob's,

will be unsettled by the fragrance.[63]

---

[63]The reference here is the Qur'an 12:94 in which Jacob claims to perceive the scent of Joseph from miles away:

"And when the caravan had departed, their father said: 'Most surely I perceive the scent of Joseph, unless you think me doting.'"

A Glance from a Friend

There is nowhere for me, O Friend,
   but in Your alley.
There is nothing in my head of worth,
   but the dust at Your door.
At the door of the tavern,
   temple, mosque and monastery,
I have fallen in prostration,
   as though You had glanced upon me.
No problem is solved in the seminary,
   and not by the speech of the sheikh.[64]
The knot of my difficulty
   would be opened by Your glance.
The Sufis and the dervishes
   present these I's and we's.
But radiance for my heart is
   Your clearing it of I's and we's.
I am nothing, nothing,
   for being is all in naught.
Nothing else but nothing,
   for You gaze upon the naught.
I followed all those of the heart,
   who head music, who had states,
But no music at the feast I heard

---

[64]The figure of the sheikh is most often used as a symbol of a rather superficial religious orthodoxy.

of the beautiful waitress.
I pray devotedly at the door of one
    who sits behind a curtain, night and day.
With just one glance from her, maybe,
    a drop will yet become a sea.

Languid Eyes

O Friend, I have become captivated
    by the mole over your lip.
I have seen your languid eyes
    and I have become sick.
I have departed from myself,
    beating the drum of "I am the Truth!"
I have become like Mansur,
    a buyer of a hanging rope.[65]
Grieving for the sweetheart
    Has cast fire in my soul,
Angry enough to die from,
and in the bazaar I am known.
Open the door of the tavern before me night and day,
for I have become weary of the mosque and seminary.
I took off the clothing of asceticism
    And of pretentiousness,
And put on the robe of the tavern's pir,[66]
    And I gained consciousness
The sermonizer in city
    Bothered me with advice,

---

[65]The reference here is to Mansur al-Hallaj, who in ecstasy said, "*Ana al-Haqq*!" (I am the Truth), and was martyred as a result in 922 C.E.

[66]A *pir* is literally an old person, but the term is typically used for a Sufi master.

Until came to my aid the breath
Of the wine drunk rouge.
Let us speak then of the temple
Of where I was awakened,
And of the idol of the tavern
By whose hand I was shaken

The sea of Annihilation [67]

If only there would come the day

when my place would be in your lane

So that my joy and sorrow there

would be my heart's exclusive care.

If only there were in my hand

* Your curl of hair with knotted strands,*

Those knots would open up for me

each complex difficulty.

Last night so far apart from you

my heart was like a darkened room

The assembly gathered 'round candle light,

of your memory burning there so bright.

When they got drunk from drinking wine,

a group of friends lost consciousness,

But of this group no share was mine,

naught for those of intelligence.

He who every bond would break

is surely unjust, ignorant, [68]

And of self and world and place

---

[67] Annihilation is *fana*, the spiritual state in which the ego is obliterated and awareness solely of God.

[68] This is a reference to Qur'an (33:72): "Surely, We offered the trust to the heaven and the mountains, but they refused to be unfaithful to it and fear from it, and man has turned unfaithful to it; surely, he is unjust, ignorant." Man is unjust to himself for taking on the burden of responsibility offered to him by God. The poet's comment is that man must be ignorant, in the sense of being heedless of worldly desire and the ego, in order to fulfill the divine trust.

he surely must be negligent.

For all those who have lost their hearts

knowledge is a curtain, a curtain,

Those who from curtains would depart,

are those whose ignorance is certain.

The lover floats upon a sea

of nothing because of zeal,

Those who in darkness stand,

are without news upon the strand.

When from the gnostic realm I come,

I saw all that had been in vain,

All that we'd heard or studies of,

was vain, after I come to love

Rajab 1405 AH (1985)

The Jug of Love

I am a supplicant for a goblet of wine
   from the hand of a sweetheart.
In whom can I confide this secret of mine,
      Where can I take this sorrow?
I have lost my soul in despair
   of seeing the face of the Friend.
I am the rue whose burnt scent fills the air;[69]
   I am the moth 'round the candle.
I have a filthy robe and prayer mat
   with which I pretend,
which at the door of the tavern
   I would rend.
From the jug of love
   just a sip from the Friend
and drunk I'll strip my soul
   from the robe of existence.
I have become old,
   but with just a glance or nod I'd be young.[70]
So, please let me go
   from the little house of the horizons.

---

[69]Literally, "I am *espand* in fire." *Espand* or *esfand* is rue, a wild herb whose seeds are burnt to
ward off the evil eye, or on occasion of happiness or sadness.

[70] Literally, a glance from the corner of the eye, idiomatically, a favor.

Good Ending

O You saqi! Fill up my cup[71]
  with wine to cleanse my soul!
For my soul is overflowing,
  flowing over with passion for fame.
Fill up my cup with the wine
  which annihilates this soul,
which expels the core of intrigue
  and my well-laid traps from being.
Fill up my cup with the wine
  which releases this soul from its own bonds,
which takes hold of my reins
  and breaks the hold of my dignity.
Fill up my cup with the wine
  which in the hideout of the rogues who know no honor
may demolish my prostrations
  and break down my standing for prayer.
I missed you in the sacred precincts
  of the flower faced girls of the tavern.
At each aperture to which I come
  another flower takes hold of my reins.
I would go to the circle of the old

---

[71]The *saqi* is the wine bearer. "O You *saqi*" is a famous phrase used in the poetry of Hafiz in which the interjection "O You" is one which occurs in numerous places in the Qur'an.

who are unconscious of themselves,

perhaps they will give me wine

   which will dispel my soul's raw thoughts.

O You Messenger! Take a message from me,

   to those who are light burdened upon the sea

of nothingness, and to the captain of the desert

   bring praises and salams from me.

I end this letter of nothing

   in nothing with a goblet!

Tell the pir of the monastery

   of this my good ending.

Ruba'iyat [Quatrains] Poetry

Precious Pearl

Fati, your nature with light is adorned!
Bonds of the intellect's veil have been shorn!
As though from an ocean of light and of grace
This precious pearl so pure has been born!

Ordibehesht 1367 AHS
[April-May 1988]

Explanation

While the above expresses something of the rhythm and
rhyme of the original, a more literal rendering of this quatrain
is as follows:

Fati, as the light of your nature adorns you
You have become beautified from the bonds of the veil of the
intellect
It is as though from the sea of the dominion of light and
eminence
This precious pearl so pure has been raised

Like so much of Imam's advice to his daughter-in-law, the
idea that intellectual pursuit can be an obstacle to communion
with one's divine nature recurs in this poem.

The words for dominion and eminence (grace), *Sultani* and
Sadr, are family names which allude to Fatimah Tabataba'i's
genealogy.

The Path

Fati who treads the path of the angelic domain
Wants to pass from the state of the noetic domain
She is blind who from the well of the sensible domain
Would go without a guide toward the divine domain

May 29, 1984

The Absolute Beauty

Fati, uproot your heart from worldly interests
Withdraw your heart from befriending this and that
Opt for only the one Friend who is the absolute beauty
Withdraw your heart from the being and space of this world

June 3, 1984

Explanation

According to the mystics of Islam, the lowest level of being is the sensible world, *nasut*. Above this is the angelic domain, *malakut*, which Henri Corbin has called the *mundis imaginalis*. Higher still is the world of the intellect, the noetic domain, *jabarut*. Finally, there is the divine domain, *lahut*.

The phrase 'being and space,' *kown o makan*, is an idiom commonly used in poetry to indicate the physical world.

74

Gnosis

Fati, what does it mean, you and the reality of gnosis
What does it mean to comprehend the essence without attributes?
Having not read the A you shall not find your way to Z
Having not read the path, what does it mean to be gifted?

The Friend

As long as you have the Friend, you shall suffer no harm,
As long as He exists, there is no dust of quality and quantity
Abandon whatever there is and choose Him
There is no advice more excellent than these two words

May 25, 1984

Wake Up

Other than the way of the Friend, where can you go?
Except for His homage, what can you say?
Whatever homage and tribute you say is His homage
Wake up, O pal, how long will you sleep?

The Sun of the World

Wake up, O friend, from this heavy sleep!
Behold the face of the beloved manifest in every particle
When you are asleep you are hidden in your selfhood
The sun of the world is hidden from your eye

June 7, 1984

Affliction of the Heart

One who is not softened by a sigh is steel hearted,
Or who is not warmed by the moaning of the heart burned,
He has cast a lasso of cruelty about his neck
The affliction of my heart causes him no shame

Sun

O sun! Rise, for we are all sleeping!
We are glowing with the fever of separation from your face
Every quarter and rooftop is enlighten by your face,
But we are like bats and are veiled

February-March 1984

A Sleeping Heart

What is the world illuminating sun compared to your eye?
Where is the memory of the face of the beloved in a sleeping
heart?[72]
With your clay body you shall not become an angel
O my friend! Where is the dust and the Lord of Lords?

---

[72]There is a saying in Arabic: *Aynaturab wa rabb al-arbab*? (Where is the dust and the Lord of Lords?) This phase is used as an exclamation to indicate infinite difference or contrast.

Wayfarer

Arise because those who tread the path are all on the way,
Constantly they move on toward the dwelling,
There, where there is no memory save that of the Friend,
The depressed hearts are all black faced

July 15, 1984

Think of a Way

If we cannot be obedient we shall sin
We shall turn from the seminary to the khanaqah[73]
The cry "I am the Truth" was the way of Mansur[74]
Oh Lord, aid me so I might think of a way

Mt. Sinai

O Friend, take me to the service of a Pir[75]
Defender, take me to be initiated[76]
My desire is to reach Mt. Sinai by this long way
Befriend me and send me a bosom friend

February-March 1985

---

[73]The *khanaqah* is the Sufi meeting place.

[74]Mansur is *Hallaj*, the martyred Sufi who was convicted of blasphemy for his utterance, "I am the Truth." See note 40, p. 30. (Eds.)

[75]A *Pir* is a Sufi master. See note 5, p. 6. (Eds.)

[76]Initiation is induction into a Sufi order.

77

Memory

To whom should I complain of separation from you?

My Defender! To whom should I go with my case against you?

The tempest of your sorrow would snap asunder the thread of existence

Your memory shall go, and I shall even forget the memory of myself

Complain

Oh Pir, I desire the khanaqah

Obedience is of no benefit, I desire sin

The companions have all departed for the Ka'bah

I complain of myself for I desire the place of sin

February-March 1985

Face of the Beloved

Oh meadow lark, get out of this cage!

Paradise seeks you, become enchanted!

You are a peacock who has come from the quarters of the beloved

Remember the face of the beloved and become mad!

78

Dervish

O you whose memory is a comfort to the hearts of the dervishes!

O you defender of the dervishes from difficulties!

There is Sinaiand the tree and there is the vision of epiphany of the face

O friends! This is what is obtained by dervishes!

March 5, 1985

No Respite

O Pir! Take me to the khanaqah!

All the companions have departed. Take me to the path

I can bear it no longer. There has come no respite

Give me refuge oh you who give aid!

Captive

It is an honor to me to become impoverished by you,

To become cut off from myself and to become your captive,

To be tempest stricken and afflicted by your dominion,

Singly to become the target of your bow and arrow

February 23, 1985

Beware

Fati! One must journey toward the Friend
One should transcend the self
Every knowledge with the scent of your being
Is a devil on the way of which one must beware

The Cup

You are not a lover if you have a name
You are not mad if you have a message
You have not tasted drunkenness if you are sober
Be gentle with us 'till you have the cup

April 29, 1984

Shadow

O charisma of Homa![77] Cast your shadow over my head!
Come to my aid, extract my existence!
The noose which has been put around my neck by desires,
Cast it round the necks of the base, O my Beloved!

---

[77]In ancient Persian legends the *Homa* is a bird, sometimes identified with the Phoenix, sometimes taken to be an osprey, which would fly over the head of a candidate to the throne and thereby bestow a kind of royal charisma upon the new king.

Hidden Cry

Who is aware of my heartache but you?
Who is with me, the madman on the roof and at the gate?
Of my interior rebellion, in whom may I confide?
Where is the heart this hidden cry affects?

March 11, 1985

Path

Open a chapter with the description of your face,
Let it begin a lock of your hair
Roll up the scroll of the science and philosophy
Cast a glance toward me, O Beloved that my path may be toward
you

A Novice of the Way

O Pir of the Way! Initiate me!
I am a novice of the Way. Be my Pir!
I am worn out; I've gotten nowhere on the path
O you beloved! Be my commander on this path[78]

March 5, 1985

---

[78] Among the Sufis the contrast between the exoteric and esoteric aspects of the religion is often spoken of as a contrast between *shari'ah* and *tariqah*. Both words literally mean a path, way or road, but the term *shari'ah* also signifies Islamic Law, while a Sufi order is referred to as a *tariqah*. Sufi initiation is called *dastgiri*, literally, taking of the hand; so, 'initiate me' could also be translated as 'take my hand,' or 'give me a hand.' The word translated here as 'novice' literally means infant, or toddler.

81

A Glance

O you my joy, my grief, my sorrow!
O my inner wound and my salve!
Cast a glance upon this worthless bit
So my banner may fly over the horizons!

Drop

I am a gnat who by your favor shall become a peacock
I am a drop from your sea, who shall become an ocean
If you show favor toward me, I shall open my wings like an
angel
I am ready to kiss the feet of the King of Tus[79]

February-March 1985

The Madman

Become mad; take off the shackles from your feet!
O peacock! Slander the raven by showing off
Don't ask the madman about the state of his heart or intellect,
Find one who is enchanted by the shackles of intellect

---

[79]The King of Tus is a reference to the eight Imam from the Prophet's progeny, Imam 'Ali ar-Rida (peace be with him), whose shrine is in Mashhad near the ancient city of Tus.

That Day

That day when I shall make my way to tavern,
I shall entrust all the friends to the Sufi robe and to the seat of the
Pir[80]
I shall tear up the scrolls of the sage, the philosopher and the
gnostic
While crying and beating my feet

March 5, 1981

The Sun's Glory

Take away the veil so you may see His beauty,
So you may see the glory of His unrivaled essence
O bat! Come out of your skin
So you may see the manifestation of the sun's glory!

Homa[81]

O peacock! Homa! Cast your shadow over my head
Befriend me and open my wings and feathers
O rescuer! Liberate me from my bonds
By your star, make my star auspicious

January-February 1985

---

[80]'Sufi robe' translates *dalq*, which is a coarse woolen garment traditionally worn by the Sufis. The
'seat of the *Pir*' is *masnad*, the place in the *khanaqah* reserved for the *Pir*, often covered by a
lambskin.

[81]See note 75, p. 67. (Eds.)

What do to?

I am Farhad,[82] I have the burning of the love of Shirin in my heart
I hope to meet my old Companion
I've lost all patience, I don't know what to do
All night I have her memory in my sorrowful heart

Thirsty for Reply

O Friend! Whatever there is, is a light from your face
The succor of this heart is your propitious glance
The night of separation came to an end, but dawn never arrived
O Beloved! The dead heart is thirsty for your reply

March 6, 1985

Quarter of the Friend

If I find a way to the quarters of the Friend,
If I find in the shelter in the shadow of her kindness,
There would be no sorrow, for the way to come and go is free.
If I am not obedient, I am a sinner

---

[82]See note 41, p. 33. (Eds.)

Your Memory

Oh! Your memory is the source of my sorrow and my joy
The cypress of your stature is the sapling of my liberation
Take away the veil from your face and open your countenance!
Oh! You are the principle of my destruction and of my flourishing

February-March 1985

Forlorn

If you are not one of the people, do not find fault with the people of the Truth
O dead ones! Do not take the living hearts to be as dead as you
Arise from this heavy sleep, O you who are forlorn!
Do not take the wakeful hearts to be in heavy sleep

Idol

With the eye of I-ness one cannot see His beauty
With the ear of thou-ness no one can hear His melody
The we-ness and thou-ness is the cause of blindness and deafness
Break this idol so that the Friend may appear!

June 23, 1984

The Holiday

This felicitous holiday is the most felicitous
The community is in the shelter of the mercy of Ahmad
On the banner of our Islamic Republic
Is the blessed portrait of Muhammad

The Banner

This felicitous holiday is the holiday of the Party of Allah
Our enemy is aware of its defeat
Because the banner of our Islamic Republic
Is preserved by the greatest name: Allah!

March 6, 1985

Explanation

These quatrains were written two weeks before the Persian New Year holiday. Ahmad is one of the names for the Prophet Muhammad (peace and blessings of Allah to him and to his progeny). The 'Party of Allah' is an expression used in the Qur'an (5:56; 58:22), in Arabic *hizbullah*:

Whoever takes as his guardian Allah and His Messenger and those who believe: indeed, the Party of Allah shall be victorious. (5:56)

Tempest

The secret of my heart is manifest to the Friend,
Along with perplexity of heart and fruitless suffering
An increasing tempest is within our hearts
O Lord! With what dust have you kneaded my clay?

Tavern

The night when all the saloons are open
The companions of the tavern sing together
Quit of the rival, beside the Beloved,
The scroll of separation closed, they share secrets

March 6, 1985

Appendix:

On the Symbolism of Religious Poetry

On the Symbolism of Religious Poetry[*]

In the Name of Allah, the Compassionate, the Merciful

Persian poetry is rich in symbolism, which may be shocking to one unfamiliar with its conventions. In the Arabic language, Sufis had already used the metaphor of intoxication for mystical experience, and of the union of lovers for the presence of God. These themes were expanded upon in Persian, and elements of pre-Islamic Persian culture were introduced to symbolize the interiorization of faith. When the Sufi poet 'Attar describes himself as a Zoroaster, he does not mean that he had abandoned Islam, but rather that there was a dimension of Islam which might appear so strange to one who was merely superficially a Muslim that it could be imagined to be a different religion. When Hafiz speaks of the hair of his beloved, he is interpreted as indicating the grace of God which emanates multiplicity, just as the strands of hair are a multiplicity. One cannot, however, simply replace the symbols of Persian poetry by their prosaic equivalents in mystical theology, for this would destroy the poem. Persian poetry derives its excitement from the impossibility of disentangling all the images, from the nagging doubt that something unorthodox lurks within it, and from the invitation of the poet to the reader to become an insider, one who sees

---

[*]Reprinted from *A Jug of Love*, op. cit., pp. 27-32. (Eds.)

91

through the apparently heretical images to the purity of the poet's meaning.

Persian poetry is the most perfect expression of the multiplicity of levels of meaning which lies at the heart of Iranian culture. Persian poetry must not be read as a puzzle to be decoded, but as an unsolvable enigma. The poetry of Imam Khomeini (may his soul be sanctified) trades on the use of the standard symbols of classical Persian mystical poetry. The apparent heterodoxy is sharpened by the position of the poet as an exoteric religious leader. Even though we know he had nothing to do with worldly wine, there is something shocking in the fact that such a person should talk about wine at all. Some have also questioned whether Islamic law does not prohibit the use of the language of love, *'ishq* in Arabic and adopted in Farsi, with reference to Allah, the Exalted.

'Ishq literally means extreme love, as has been mentioned in the standard dictionaries of classical Arabic. Sometimes it has been defined as "exceeding the limits of love". One must not assume, however, that this refers to physical passion and carnal desires, for the expression has a more general meaning, and a profusion of love with respect to anything may be called *'ishq*.

Love is one of the most elevated sentiments of the heart, which in its pure essence, according to the Muslim mystics and philosophers, is free from the incidental impurity of the carnal soul. If in some cases love accompanies such impurities

92

it is not necessary that at all stages it should do so. The mystics of Islam, the '*urafa*, even go so far as to say that it is incorrect to use the term '*ishq* for the physical passions, because passion is only something that happens to accompany love in some cases. Since love is not to be confused with passion, which is not included in the literal meaning of '*ishq*, if '*ishq* is used for carnal desire it must be understood as a figurative use of the word if it is allowed at all. Thus, the mystics reverse the claim made by many Western as well as Eastern commentators on mystical poetry, that the language of love is applied to God only figuratively. Such commentators assume that the literal meaning of such language is for something physical, but by attending to the meaning of the words used we see that love must be understood as something essentially spiritual.

One might object that if love is not to be interpreted as necessarily physical, neither must it be interpreted to be essentially spiritual, but should be neutral with regard to the material and the spiritual. A moment's reflection, however, suffices to realize that whatever is considered to be of such a nature that it may or may not have a physical aspect must be regarded as spiritual, for it is the nature of spirit to be contingently associated with the body in this way.

The mystics and philosophers for centuries have taught that the demands of the carnal soul are ever perishing and evanescent. What is called 'carnal love' originates from the sexual instinct, and it must not be confused with the reality of the spiritual sentiment. Carnal love is like the other animal instincts. *'Ishq*, however, is said to become a part of the human nature itself and not to perish.

Intense love, wherever, it is found, can be correctly designated by the word *'ishq*. For example, one may speak of the word *'ishq* of the mother for her children or their love for her; one may speak of even higher stages of *'ishq* for the most lofty human sentiments, like *'ishq* for knowledge or *'ishq* for service to society, and all are correct. Hence, the application of the word *'ishq* to God in such poetry as that of Hafiz or Imam Khomeini, or in the writings of the mystics should not be viewed with suspicion and must be considered perfectly permissible from a religious point of view.

Furthermore, in the noble Qur'an it has been said: "Those who believe have intense love for Allah" (*wal-ladhina amanu ashaddu hubban lillah*) (2:165). Intense love is nothing but *'ishq*, as has been reported in the dictionaries. This word also occurs in *hadiths*. *Kulayni*, for example, narrates from the sixth Imam, peace be with him, that he said:

> "The Prophet (s) said, 'The best of people is one who loves (*'ishq*) worship, embraces it, loves (*hubb*) it with his whole heart, and occupies his body with it, and prepares for it, and he does not care whether he has comfort or trouble in this world.'"

The use of the word *'ishq* in this *hadith* provides positive proof that the meaning of *'ishq* is not restricted to passionate affairs, nor even to material affairs. Of course, the application of the term, Beloved (*ma'shuq*), for God as a Name is forbidden and is considered incorrect by the scholars of Islamic law, for the divine Names are fixed (*tawfiqi*). One should only consider terms to be Names of God when this is expressly indicated by God Himself through the revelation to His prophets. This is different, however, from the use of such a term not as a Name of God, but as an adjective when it is not intended as a Name of God, as in poetry and mystical expressions, and as such it poses no difficulty from the point of view of Islamic law. The meaning of 'the Beloved' and 'Friend' is also found in the following hadith *qudsi*:

"When a servant is occupied completely with My service I will make his desire and pleasure to be remembering Me. Whenever I make his desire and pleasure to be in remembering Me, he will love Me and I will love him, and when he loves Me and I love him, I will remove the veil from that which is between Me and him."

There are several other hadiths like this in which the word '*ishq* or its cognates appears. Shaykh Abu'l-Muhasan Husayn ibn Hasan Jorjani in his *Tafsir Jala'al-Adhhan wa Jala'al-Ahzan,* known as *Tafsir-e Gazor*, commenting on the significance of the letters *Ha Mim 'Ayn Sin Qaf,* says that some say that this ayah is about the dignity of the Prophet, may the peace and blessings of Allah be with him and his progeny. "Ha is the pool (*hawd*) of entrance, *Mim* is the kingdom (*mulk*) of expanse, '*Ayn* is the love ('*ishq*) of the

95

Worshipped and the highness (*'uluww*) of limitlessness, Sin is the visible brilliance (*sana'*), Qaf is his standing (*qa'im*) in a praiseworthy position (*maqam*) and his nearness (*qurbat*) to the generosity of the worshipped..." in which sentence the phrase *'ishq* for the Worshipped is mentioned.

Some object to the use of the word *'ishq* because it is not used in the Qur'an, but there are many words which are current among legal scholars of Islam that are not used in the Qur'an, such as the word *ijtihad*, the use of which is unproblematic, and on this matter there is no disagreement. Hence the use of the *'ishq* by the mystics and poets should not be a source of any doubts about religious propriety.

The method of poetry involves taking liberties with language, and using images, sounds and rhythms, and other techniques, such as allusion to the writings of earlier poets. All of this is to be found in the poetry of Imam Khomeini, may Allah pour light into his grave, as well. Sometimes allusion is made to shocking behavior, or there may appear to be an apparently disrespectful attitude displayed for the mosque or the seminary, but disrespect and indulgence of sinful behavior are far from the poet's intention, which, if one looks below the surface, can be seen to be the expression of intense love for Allah.

Index

About the Translators

Dr. Ghulam-RidaA'wani heads the Iranian Academy of Philosophy in Tehran. He also teaches Islamic Philosophy at Shahid Beheshti University and the University of Tehran. Dr. A'wani has authored and edited numerous books on Islamic philosophy and mysticism, including *40 Poems from the Divan of Nasir ad-Din Khosrow,* co-edited and co-translated with Peter Wilson. He received his Ph.D. from the University of Tehran.

Dr. Muhammad G. Legenhausen is a research fellow at the Iranian Academy of Philosophy in Tehran. He has taught philosophy at Rice University and at Texas Southern University. He has published various articles on metaphysics and the philosophy of religion, and is the co-editor with Mahdi 'Abidi of *Jihad and Shahadat: Struggle and Martyrdom in Islam.* He received his Ph.D. in philosophy from Rice University.

An Introduction of the Institute for Compilation and Publication of Imam Khomeini's Works

The splendor of the Islamic Revolution and the role of Imam Khomeini's personality, views, thoughts, and literary works in the occurrence and perpetuity of the Revolution; the need of the future generation for the works of the founder of the Islamic Republic and standard-bearer of the global Islamic movement; the publication and propagation of the authentic and complete works and thoughts of His Eminence; and the prevention of historical distortion of the Islamic Revolution were among the factors which prompted Hujjat al-Islam wal-Muslimin Haj Sayyid Ahmad Khomeini to inquire through an elaborate letter about His Eminence's view on the manner of studying, compiling and publishing his own works and related documents, and to determine the authority in supervising and ascertaining the authenticity or otherwise of whatever is to be published in the name of Imam Khomeini both in Iran and abroad. In his reply in the form of a written decree dated September 8, 1988 (Shahrivar 17, 1367 AHS), His Eminence assigned the responsibility of compilation and collection of all materials relevant to him to his own son, Haj Sayyid Ahmad.

In consonance with this decree, the Institute for Compilation and Publication of Imam Khomeini's Works was established and has commenced its activities. The heart-rending event of the demise of the Imam of the Muslims and the burgeoning need of the Islamic society to obtain His Eminence's guidelines and literary works have compelled this Institute to expand its realm of activities qualitatively and quantitatively. Along this line, the law on the preservation of Imam Khomeini's works was enacted by the Islamic Consultative Assembly (the Iranian Parliament) on

November 5, 1989 (Aban 14, 1368 AHS) and approved by the Council of Guardians as binding and ready for execution. In this manner, pursuant to its momentous religious and legal mission, this Institute has embarked on planning and modifying its organizational structure within the framework of the following objectives:

1. Collection of all related documents and literary works of Imam Khomeini as well as all works relevant to his personality, life, struggles, and thoughts written by writers or made by artists both in Iran and abroad;

2. Permanent preservation of the aforementioned documents and works through the most appropriate means;

3. Study and research on the literary works for the elucidation of the history of the Islamic Revolution, Imam Khomeini biography, and compilation, translation and preparation of the literary works' compendium for publication;

4. Publication of the literary works' compendium through various means both in Iran and abroad, and propagation and dissemination of the Imam's thoughts and ideals;

5. Perpetual supervision of everything written or made by artists in the name of Imam Khomeini; prevention of distortion of the Imam's speeches, writings, and events related to the Imam; giving replies to the inquirers and researchers on the literary works as the official center for the collection and preservation of the documents and works of the Imam. In order to attain the above-cited objectives, the main programs and activities of this Institute can be divided into the following five areas:

a. Collection of the documents and works, which include
(i) collection of documents and works of Imam Khomeini;
(ii) collection of all works related to the Imam's

biography, struggles and thoughts written or made both in Iran and abroad;

b. Permanent preservation of the documents and works;

c. Study and research, translation, compilation, and preparation of the works for publication;

d. Publication of the works and continuous revival and propagation of the thoughts and school of thought of Imam Khomeini;

e. Supervision: Consonant with the decree of the Imam and enactment of the Islamic Consultative Assembly, the Institute is the sole official source of whatever is to be published in the name of Imam Khomeini.

List of English Publications
(August 2002)

The following list of English publications of the Institute for Compilation and Publication of Imam Khomeini's Works are available free on request:

• A Call to Divine Unity: Imam Khomeini's Letter to Mikhail Gorbachev, Leader of the Soviet Union
• Father! O Standard Bearer of Islam
• Imam Khomeini and the Culture of 'Ashura: Abstracts of Papers Presented at the International Congress on Imam Khomeini and the Culture of 'Ashura
• Kauthar: An Anthology of Imam Khomeini's Speeches Including an Account of the Events of the Islamic Revolution (1962-1978) (3 Volumes)
• Pithy Aphorisms
• Standpoints: A Selection of Stances Assumed by Hujjat al-Islam wal-Muslimin Haj Sayyid Ahmad Khomeini
• The 'Ashura Uprising
• The Last Message: Imam Khomeini's Religio-Political Testament
• Palestine from Imam Khomeini's Viewpoint
• Hajj in the Words and Messages of Imam Khomeini
• The Narrative of Awakening: A Glance at Imam Khomeini's Ideal, Scientific and Political Biography (2nd Edition)
• Fundamentals of the Islamic Revolution: Selections from the Thoughts and Opinions of Imam Khomeini

- Imam Khomeini on Exportation of Revolution
- The Life of Imam Khomeini (Volume 1)
- The Position of Women from the Viewpoint of Imam Khomeini
- Islamic Government: Governance of the Jurist
- Adab as-Salat: The Disciplines of the Prayer (2nd Edition)
- Reunion with the Beloved: Imam Khomeini's Letters to Hujjat al-Islam wal-Muslimin Haj Sayyid Ahmad Khomeini (2nd Edition)
- The Greatest Jihad: Combat with the Self
- The Wine of Love: Mystical Poetry of Imam Khomeini
- Forty Hadiths: An Exposition of Mystical and Ethical Traditions (forthcoming)
- Sahifeh-ye Imam: An Anthology of Imam Khomeini's Speeches, Messages, Interviews, Decrees, Religious Permissions, and Letters (22 Volumes) (forthcoming)

Kindly address your request for these books as well as for others in more than 20 different languages of the world to the International Affairs Department, The Institute for Compilation and Publication of Imam Khomeini's Works, P.O. Box 19575/614, Tehran, Islamic Republic of Iran, or e-mail: info@imam-khomeini.org.